July 12.

HIS DISCIPLES
BELIEVED
IN HIM

Devotional Readings on the Gospel of John

PASTOR REA GRANT

xulon
PRESS

HIS DISCIPLES BELIEVED IN HIM
Devotional Readings on the Gospel of John
by Pastor Rea Grant

Printed in the United States of America

ISBN 9781498409490

Scripture quotations taken from NIV – UK Copyright © 2011

www.xulonpress.com

DEDICATION

Soli Deo Gloria

This book is dedicated to
the life and ministry of

ROBERT ANDREW BOGGS

a faithful servant of God whom he served
for over 40 years as the beloved pastor of

TOBERMORE BAPTIST CHURCH
and an earnest preacher of the Gospel.

'Well done, good and faithful servant'
Matthew 25:23

'His disciples believed in him'

DEVOTIONAL READINGS IN THE GOSPEL OF JOHN

It was a long time ago when, as a young teenager, I began to read my Bible seriously. I ask you to imagine how puzzled I was to read in John 2:11 that following Jesus' first miracle in Cana of Galilee, *'his disciples believed in him.'*

It seemed a strange thing to say about disciples of Jesus. Didn't they already believe in him, and if not, why had they followed him?

I know by now that their knowledge of Jesus took a huge step forward that day as they saw his glory, and laid hold of a fuller revelation of him than they had ever experienced before. I also know by now that every believer needs to grow like this. What better way can there be than by reading the life of Jesus Christ as it is recorded in the gospels?

I have chosen John 2:11 as an appropriate title for this book
HIS DISCIPLES BELIEVED IN HIM.

It is my hearty prayer that heaven will record that wherever this book is read by believers around the world *'his disciples believed in him.'*

I cannot begin to list all those preachers and teachers whose ministry down the years have moulded my thinking about John's Gospel but I would like to tell you about two such men.

The first was one of my lecturers at Belfast Bible College. He lectured us on John's Gospel one year and on Jeremiah the following year. It is not an exaggeration to say that we would not have been surprised to meet either John or Jeremiah at the local bus stop, and we would have recognised them immediately. His name was Mr. Hugh T. Combe, who lectured in Stranmillis College of Education, Belfast (as it was then known). Alongside his considerable expertise in mathematics he voluntarily made a great contribution to the spiritual development of several generations of students at Belfast Bible College. Another memory is that while we were busy trying to capture the final sentences of his lecture, he would already have picked up his satchel and notes and taken a few quiet steps to the lecture room door. Just as he was disappearing he would say 'For next week explain, illustrate and apply – and then he would add a text or passage of scripture – and with that he was gone. That formula 'explain, illustrate and apply' has stood me in good stead for 54 years.

The other man to whom I owe a great debt is well-known around the world far beyond his native Scotland. He is Dr. Bruce Milne, who having served several of the churches of the Baptist Union of Scotland, moved to become Senior Minister of First Baptist Church, Vancouver, Canada. I contacted him in the course of writing this book. Among his many achievements he wrote a wonderful commentary entitled *'The Message of John'* in The Bible Speaks Today series (Inter Varsity Press 1993). I had read widely on John's writings but it was only when I came across Bruce's book I realised I had found 'the key that fitted the lock'. If he ever gets round to reading this book, he may recognise the flourish of his pen here and there. If so, I hope he feels rewarded. I pray God's richest blessing for Bruce and his wife, now in retirement.

Personal Bible Reading

Probably the majority of Bible readers follow the chapter divisions of the Bible. It is better doing this, than not reading the Bible at all. Reading the Bible all by yourself is interesting and useful, but if this is all you do, simply read a passage and close the book, it can become unproductive and boring, and soon you may stop reading the Bible altogether.

This is why at the end of each study in this book you will find an item with the title *'Thank You, Heavenly Father.'* The themes for thanksgiving and praise that follow all arise from the chapter section you were reading before closing your Bible.

We need to think about what we read. Most of us find the concentration that this requires is the difficult part of this otherwise good, personal, daily habit.

So we may begin casting around for a larger book that will help us get to grips with the contents of a Bible book. A Bible Dictionary and Handbook is a very useful thing to have. Ask about this in your Bible bookshop, or discuss the matter with other believers, and guidance will come. However a bigger book than the one you have in your hand is, by itself, not the answer. The basic issue is: are you willing to read your Bible, asking God the Holy Spirit to open your eyes to its truth?

The Signs in John's Gospel

John's gospel is long, and the material he included is arranged differently to the Synoptic Gospels. There are reasons for this that are straightforward. John the apostle, who at one time was the youngest disciple of Jesus wrote this gospel many years after the other writers. It is thought that he wrote the gospel between 90 and 100 AD. He had lived to be the oldest of the apostles.

So John wrote his gospel for the instruction and guidance of the numerous churches that had sprung up around the Mediterranean world as the result of apostolic preaching and itinerant evangelism.

John's Gospel has two parts.
Chapters 1 to 12 are about Jesus' public ministry.
Chapters 13 to 21 are about Jesus' ministry to his own.

Back to chapters 1 – 12. Follow me closely and you will discover that these chapters have a backbone that is easily recognised once it is pointed out. John had collected a number of **'signs'** (or miracles of Jesus), all of which are found in chapters 1 – 12. So one way of navigating through these chapters is to look out for the signs/miracles and take your bearings from them. Now, I hope you want to know where to find them.

The First Sign   At Cana in Galilee   2:1-11
The Second Sign   Healing the Official's Son   4:43-54
The Third Sign   Healing the Lame Man   5:15

The Fourth Sign	Feeding the Five Thousand	6:1-15
The Fifth Sign	Walking on the Water	6:16-24
The Sixth Sign	Healing the Blind Man	9:1-41
The Seventh Sign	The Raising of Lazarus	11:1-57

You will find out that the signs are interspersed
with numerous other events in Jesus' ministry.

Finally I must record thanks to my valued friend James
Greenwood, who painstakingly proof reads my work. I think
I would like to have been one of his students at Stranmillis
Teacher Training College, Belfast when he was on the staff
there. Working with him is a rich and stimulating experience.
It's never too late to learn from a good man.

Your friend in Christ,
Rea Grant
January 2015

LIST OF CONTENTS
Introductory Comments on Chapters 1 to 12

Chapter 1

John 1:1-18

THE WORD BECAME FLESH

The Gospel of John has a majestic and impressive opening sentence. We can set it alongside Moses' opening sentence in the Book of Genesis. One text says 'Amen' to the other.

In the beginning God created the heavens and the earth. Genesis 1:1

In the beginning was the Word, and the Word was with God, and the Word was God. He was with God in the beginning. John 1:1-2

Moses began his book of beginnings at Creation, with God, on the threshold of history. John began his gospel in eternity, before history, with God. John presents the truth without apology, without hesitation, without any doubt, and his readers are left to believe it or not as they will. If they want to know more, then they are at liberty to read on.

Dr. Alexander MacLaren (1826-1910), is remembered for his notable pastorate in Manchester, England. Generations of preachers have been grateful for his Bible commentaries. Introducing the Gospel of John he wrote:

> *'The other gospels begin with Bethlehem; John begins in the bosom of the Father. Luke dates his narrative by Roman emperors and Jewish High Priests; John dates his 'in the beginning'. Matthew and Luke take us to the cradle and the manger, Mark to Old Testament prophecies, but John takes us into the mists of eternity.'*

> *'John used a larger canvas and broad strokes in order to take our minds and hearts where they have never been before, enabling us to see Jesus 'as he really is' in the context of eternity and history.'*

Reading through John's prologue to his gospel is like standing in a vast cathedral 'with a crick in your neck' as your eye follows the soaring arches in stone and wood above and around you. You ask yourself how the workmen in those days could turn out such splendid work using only very primitive tools. A similar thought comes to mind as we read these eighteen verses: and conclude very quickly that there was someone helping John to write what he wanted to say, using words that are both simple and profound. Yes, John's helper was the Holy Spirit.

Can we find words to help us remember the many fine and true things about Jesus that are recorded here? We can only try.

Jesus Christ in relation to God vv. 1-2

Jesus is ETERNAL: 'In the beginning was the Word;' he shared God's eternality.

Jesus is DISTINCT: 'And the Word was with God;' not to be confused with the Father and the Holy Spirit.

Jesus is DIVINE: 'And the Word was God;' a full member of the Godhead, sharing all the attributes of God. One in Godhead with the Father and the Holy Spirit.

Jesus is CHANGELESS: The Word of God revealed here on the threshold of history 'is still the same today'. Hebrews 13:8

Jesus is INFINITE AND LIMITLESS: He is GOD. Can we know a God as big as this? Yes we can. That is why John wrote his gospel.

Jesus Christ and the created universe vv. 3-5

³Through him all things were made; without him nothing was made that has been made. ⁴In him was life, and that life was the light of all mankind. ⁵The light shines in the darkness, and the darkness has not overcome it. 1:3-5

The Word who is God created all things. v. 3

Notice the emphasis in this statement. There were and are no exceptions to all things that were made. God the Word made them all.

God the Father, God the Word and God the Holy Spirit are distinct from the created world and existed prior to everything else. Recall Paul explaining the Christian view of God in 1 Cor. 8:4-6.

The Shorter Catechism of the Westminster Assembly asks the question

Q. 6 How many persons are there in the Godhead?

A. There are three persons in the Godhead; the Father, the Son and the Holy Spirit, and these three are one God, the same in essence, equal in power and glory.

So far as John is concerned the deeds and words of Jesus are the deeds and words of God.

The Word is the source of Life and Light. v.4

Before the initial action of speaking the world out of nothing, the person who is God the Word possessed the attributes of life and light. All life derives from him. All light comes from him.

The handiwork of God the Word in Creation stands forever as a visual aid to mankind about the existence and power of God.

The light of Jesus brings light to every human being. v. 4

The light shines in the context of darkness.

The darkness has not overcome it (i.e. put it out).

Jesus' attributes of light and life make it possible for people like us to know God. It was for this purpose that John wrote his gospel: 20:39 & 21:25

Jesus Christ and the gospel story vv. 6-8

⁶There was a man sent from God whose name was John. ⁷He came as a witness to testify concerning that light, so that through him all might believe. ⁸He himself was not the light; he came only as a witness to the light. 1:6-8

The Ministry of John the Baptist

All the Gospel writers and apostolic preachers consistently see John the Baptist as the immediate starting point of Jesus' ministry.

He is described as a witness: (martyr) a title that belongs to all Christians. As such John was a model. Herod had him beheaded. He had a sense of personal mission: he was sent from God. v. 6 His ministry had a specific purpose, no less that winning his hearers to personal faith in Jesus, that through him all men might believe. v. 7

He had a Christ-centred message: a witness to the light. v. 8 John did not in any way, either by word or action, confuse his hearers. He himself was not that light. He was first and always a witness to the light.

The coming of God the Word into the world vv. 9-14

⁹The true light that gives light to everyone was coming into the world. ¹⁰He was in the world, and though the world was made through him, the world did not recognise him. ¹¹He came to that which was his own, but his own did not receive him. ¹²Yet to all who did receive him, to those who believed in his name, he gave the right to become children of God – ¹³children born not of natural descent, nor of human decision or a husband's will, but born of God. ¹⁴The Word became flesh and made his dwelling among us. We have seen his glory, the glory of the one and only Son, who came from the Father, full of grace and truth. 1:9-14

The light that was coming into the world was a Person, a Divine Person, none other than God the Word. If the truth were told, every human being would confess that 'GOD IS.' Hebrews 11:6. No matter how deprived, depraved, defiled or dull the human conscience may become, the ability to 'know with' (*con-science*) comes from God the Word.

When the Gospel is preached God the Word illumines the mind and conscience of the hearer, so that they can comprehend and accept the life.

> *[10]He was in the world, and though the world was made through him, the world did not recognise him. [11]He came to that which was his own, but his own did not receive him.* 1:10-11

These verses record a great tragedy (v. 10) i.e. his own people did not know him.' Verse 11 records an even deeper tragedy: he was the Messiah of Israel, but his own heritage did not receive him. The coming of the Word into the world was met with ignorance.

Verse 12 contains the very best of news. This is the gospel of Jesus Christ.

> *[12]Yet to all who did receive him, to those who believed in his name, he gave the right to become children of God – [13]children born not of natural descent, nor of human* decision *or a husband's will, but born of God.* 1:12-13

Notice three things about people who accepted Jesus:

They received him.

They believed in his name.

They were born of God.

The term 'believed' in occurs here for the first time in this gospel. John the apostle doesn't want us to believe about Jesus. He wants us to believe in/on Jesus.

This faith isn't an easy-believism. The repentant sinner turning to Jesus in faith throws himself on his Lord and only Saviour.

We accept that Jesus *is* who He claims to be,

and dedicate our lives to Him.

Here is the whole Bible story encapsulated in the space of a single verse:

> *[14]The Word became flesh and made his dwelling among us. We have seen his glory, the glory of the one and only Son, who came from the Father, full of grace and truth.* 1:14

Of all the statements that John has made so far in his gospel this is a very rich one. Think of who the Word is, what the Word did, and why He did it.

Jesus Christ left the glory of heaven, and was born by natural birth to his mother Mary and lived among us for over 30 years. During that time, and particularly in the events of his passion and crucifixion, death and burial, he revealed the glory of God to a sinful world. That glory still shines as we read the gospel story.

Is there anywhere in the world's literature a more significant and memorable sentence than John 1:14? It is the key that unlocks the mystery of Christ, it is the heart and climax of the gospel.

This is the point at which Christianity parts company with all non-Christian thought. The Word, agent of Creation has become a creature.

The Word became 'flesh'. That word 'flesh' stands for the whole person.

Here is Jesus, the divine Logos, one with the Father in divinity (v. 1) and one with us in humanity (v. 14)

There will be no going-back on the Incarnation. It is a completed act of God. He is eternally 'God with us'. No other can stand alongside him or take his place.

The coming of the Word in human flesh does not save us in itself – the DEATH of the GOD-MAN is also required as John will make clear later.

God used to live among his people in the Tabernacle in the wilderness – but a new era has begun. He now lives in the person of his Son. The words for 'dwell and 'tent' are derived from the Hebrew word 'Shekinah' the term that referred to God's glorious presence in the midst of his people.

Hence without hesitation John goes on to write
WE HAVE SEEN HIS GLORY.

There are five verses remaining and these are the conclusion to this thrilling study.

The testimony of the Apostles vv.14b-18

[14]The Word became flesh and made his dwelling among us. We have seen his glory, the glory of the one and only Son, who came from the Father, full of grace and truth. 1:14

We already spent some time in v. 14 – and we could stay there for a week! But we must move on.

[15](John testified concerning him. He cried out, saying, 'This is the one I spoke about when I said, "He who comes after me has surpassed me because he was before me."') 1:15

V. 15 is a further imprimatur from John the Baptist. John the Apostle recalls it and adds it to the evidence of all the apostles.

[16]Out of his fullness we have all received grace in place of grace already given. [17]For the law was given through Moses; grace and truth came through Jesus Christ. 1:16-17

V. 16 is a marvellous testimony to the grace of our Lord Jesus Christ. It is in fact the unanimous testimony of the entire apostolic band.

The expression *'grace in place of grace already given'* is interesting. Did a milkman ever call at your home delivering milk? Your mother put out empty bottles at the front doorstep at bedtime. Lo and behold, next morning, they had been replaced by full ones.

Next time you are on holiday by the sea. Stand for a while at the edge of the tide. Allow it to drive you up back up the beach – or else ebb away from you. Tide after tide comes and goes. That is how God's grace comes to us. Every day. Day by day.

[18]No one has ever seen God, but the one and only Son, who is himself God and is in the closest relationship with the Father, has made him known. 1:18

Apart from Peter, James and John with Jesus on the Mount of Transfiguration had mortal eye ever before gazed on the glory of God in the face of Jesus Christ?

WE KNOW GOD TODAY – BECAUSE HE HAS MADE HIMSELF KNOWN TO US IN HIS SON JESUS.

Thank You, Heavenly Father:

For Your immeasurable gift to mankind in the incarnation of Your Son Jesus;

For Your meticulous planning in bringing him safely into the world from the womb of his mother Mary;

For the parental care that Mary and Joseph gave him; for Your protection of the family when Your Son's life was threatened;

For your choice of Mary and Joseph as guardians of Your One and Only Son;

For the song that is in our hearts as we meditate on the incarnation of Jesus: *'Worthy O Lamb of God art Thou, that every knee to Thee shall bow.'*

In Jesus' Name, Amen

John 1:19-34

THE ROLE OF JOHN THE BAPTIST IN THE MINISTRY OF JESUS

¹⁹Now this was John's testimony when the Jewish leaders in Jerusalem sent priests and Levites to ask him who he was. ²⁰He did not fail to confess, but confessed freely, 'I am not the Messiah.'
1:19-20

John the Baptist was a phenomenon in Israel in his day. He was the last of the Old Testament prophets and the first witness to the coming of the Messiah and Redeemer. We recall John's involvement in Jesus' baptism in the River Jordan. Luke 3:21-22. We also recall how Jesus publicly commended John's ministry. Matthew 11:7-19.

With the arrival of John on the public scene in Israel the long inter-testament silence was broken and the prophetic word was again being heard in the land. The evidence says that his preaching stirred up great excitement in his hearers and had a marked impact on them.

In this section (1:19-28) the Jews have sent no less than two deputations to question him: priests and Levites in vv. 19-23 and Pharisees in vv. 24-27. In reply to the priests and Levites John made it clear that he was not 'the Christ' and he was not Elijah. John 1. 19-21

> *²¹They asked him, 'Then who are you? Are you Elijah?' He said,
> 'I am not.'*
> *'Are you the Prophet?' He answered, 'No.'*
> *²²Finally they said, 'Who are you? Give us an answer to take back
> to those who sent us. What do you say about yourself?'*
> *²³John replied in the words of Isaiah the prophet, 'I am the voice
> of one calling in the wilderness, "Make straight the way for the
> Lord."* 1:21-23

We recognise John's quotation from Isaiah 40:3-5 in his
answer to the Jews. John was of no importance. The important
thing was that he was 'a voice' preparing the way of the Lord.
In reply to a question about his practice of baptising (vv. 14-28)
he had a forthright answer.

> *²⁴Now the Pharisees who had been sent ²⁵questioned him, 'Why
> then do you baptise if you are not the Messiah, nor Elijah, nor the
> Prophet?' ²⁶'I baptise with water,' John replied, 'but among you
> stands one you do not know. ²⁷He is the one who comes after me,
> the straps of whose sandals I am not worthy to untie.'*
> *²⁸This all happened at Bethany on the other side of the Jordan,
> where John was baptising.* 1:24-28

The Bethany mentioned in v. 28 was not where Mary and
Martha and Lazarus lived. It was near Jerusalem.

In things that were trivial John left the people wondering – he
wasn't going to waste time or be diverted from his main task
of representing Jesus. In important matters he did his utmost to
remove any misunderstanding that might have been in the people's minds, about his identity for example.

Jesus the Lamb of God who takes away the sin of the world
John testifies about Jesus vv. 29-34

[29]The next day John saw Jesus coming towards him and said, 'Look, the Lamb of God, who takes away the sin of the world! 1:29

It will help us to realise that John the Apostle was not attempting to give us daily accounts of where Jesus had been or what he had said or done. He leaves us to wonder about that.

In fact verses 32-34 are evidence that the baptism of Jesus and his temptation in the wilderness have taken place. If so, then it is possible that this is where Jesus was returning from the wilderness in the fullness of the Holy Spirit, intent on fulfilling his ministry. John plunges right into telling us about this.

[29]The next day John saw Jesus coming towards him and said, 'Look, the Lamb of God, who takes away the sin of the world!' [30]This is the one I meant when I said, "A man who comes after me has surpassed me because he was before me." [31]I myself did not know him, but the reason I came baptising with water was that he might be revealed to Israel.'
[32]Then John gave this testimony: 'I saw the Spirit come down from heaven as a dove and remain on him. [33]And I myself did not know him, but the one who sent me to baptise with water told me, "The man on whom you see the Spirit come down and remain is the one who will baptise with the Holy Spirit." [34]I have seen and I testify that this is God's Chosen One.' 1:29-34

John made three points about Jesus in his preaching:
(1) That Jesus is the Lamb of God, who takes away the sin of the world (v. 29)
(2) That Jesus surpassed John because He was pre-existent (v.30)

(3) That the descent of the Holy Spirit on Jesus at his baptism was divine confirmation that He is the Son of God (vv. 32-34).

John had no hesitation in adding his testimony at this point; he both witnessed the descent of the Spirit on Jesus and understood what it signified.

Which Old Testament Lamb was John thinking about when he spoke about Jesus as the Lamb of God? This is not clear, but there is a biblical emphasis in his words: lit. *'The Lamb of God's providing.'*

1st Immediately our minds go back to the ram caught in the thicket which Abram took and offered in place of Isaac in Genesis 22. Isaac had asked his father Abram: *'The fire and the wood are here but where is the lamb for the burnt offering?'*

Abraham answered, *'God himself will provide a Lamb for the burnt offering, my son.'*

There are other possibilities:

2nd John was familiar with the prophecy of Isaiah and would have known chapter 53. In vv. 4-6 Jesus is said to have carried our sins which his Father laid on him:

'Surely he took up our pain and bore our suffering, yet we considered him punished by God, stricken by him, and afflicted. 5But he was pierced for our transgressions, he was crushed for our iniquities; the punishment that brought us peace was on him, and by his wounds we are healed. We all, like sheep, have gone astray, each of us has turned to our own way; and the Lord has laid on him the iniquity of us all. Isaiah 53:4-6

3rd There is an even clearer picture provided by the Day of Atonement in Israel. Two lambs would be selected; one to die on the altar of sacrifice, and the other known as the scapegoat, over which the High Priest confessed the sins of the people, was led away into the wilderness—a rather vivid illustration of a lamb taking away the sins of the people.

We are not told where this preaching took place or who the people in the audience were.

John 1. 35-51

JOHN'S DISCIPLES FOLLOW JESUS

From here to the end of the chapter we are introduced to men 'who received Him' (in the words of v. 12).

From vv. 35-42 Jesus is involved with two of John the Baptist's disciples: one of them is Andrew and the other is the apostle John himself.

Yesterday the two disciples received the information that Jesus was 'the Lamb of God, who takes away the sin of the world.' (v. 29)

Today it seems the Baptist and his two other disciples observed Jesus passing by: and for a second time the Baptist identified Jesus as the Lamb of God. (v. 35) Today, the two men. Andrew and John, will take the decisive step that they will remember for the rest of their lives.

> *37When the two disciples heard him say this, they followed Jesus.*
> *38Turning round, Jesus saw them following and asked, 'What do you want?'*
> *They said, 'Rabbi' (which means 'Teacher'), 'where are you staying?'*
> *39Come,' he replied, 'and you will see.'*
> *So they went and saw where he was staying, and they spent that day with him. It was about four in the afternoon. 1:37-39*

So while the bulk of the people did not believe in Jesus, there were exceptions who believed in him and found eternal life.

John presents this week in Jesus' life as spent mainly in making disciples. He took the initiative in gaining disciples. The Christian church knows these two men because of the witness of the New Testament scriptures to their service as apostles of Jesus Christ. But until Jesus called them and they followed him, they were nobodies!

The calling of Andrew 1:40-41

40Andrew, Simon Peter's brother, was one of the two who heard what John had said and who had followed Jesus. 1:40

It is interesting to note that the calling of these disciples began with the repetition of Jesus' title spoken by the Baptist: *'Look, the Lamb of God.'* The likelihood is that John the Apostle is reminding his readers that *following Jesus begins with recognition of Him as Saviour.*

The calling of Peter 1:42

The first thing Andrew did was to find his brother Simon and tell him, "We have found the Messiah" (that is, the Christ). And he brought him to Jesus. Jesus looked at him and said, "You are Simon son of John. You will be called Cephas" (which, when translated, is Peter). 1:41-42

Thank God for enthusiasm! There was an overflow from Andrew's coming to Jesus: *'the first thing Andrew did was to find his brother Simon and tell him, "We have found the Messiah (that is, the Christ)."*

Immediately Andrew introduced his brother Simon to Jesus he became the subject of a prophecy made by Jesus: *"You are SIMON son of John. You will be called CEPHAS" (which, when translated, is PETER).* The name Peter means 'A ROCK.' *Jesus addressed Simon in terms of the person he was to become.* Jesus saw great spiritual potential in this man.

The calling of Philip 1:43-45

The next day Jesus decided to leave for Galilee. Finding Philip, he said to him, "Follow me." Philip, like Andrew and Peter, was from the town of Bethsaida. 1:43-44

Philip is not a stranger to modern believers. However he was one of the less prominent of the disciples. He was a calculating individual (John 6:5-7), good at mental arithmetic!

He may have been a man of limited initiative: if Jesus had not taken the initiative in calling him, would he have joined his friends in following Jesus?

Nevertheless Philip shows himself to be an effective personal witness as he points his friend Nathaniel to Christ. Vv. 45-51

The calling of Nathaniel 1:45-51

Philip found Nathanael and told him, "We have found the one Moses wrote about in the Law, and about whom the prophets also wrote—Jesus of Nazareth, the son of Joseph."
"Nazareth! Can anything good come from there?" Nathanael asked.
"Come and see," said Philip.
When Jesus saw Nathanael approaching, he said of him, "Here is a true Israelite, in whom there is no deceit."
"How do you know me?" Nathanael asked. Jesus answered, "I saw you while you were still under the fig-tree before Philip called you."

Then Nathanael declared, "Rabbi, you are the Son of God; you are the King of Israel." 1:45-51

Nathaniel too, had a *'canny'* side to him. Listen to Philip telling him about Jesus: "We have found the one Moses wrote about in the Law, and about whom the prophets also wrote—Jesus of Nazareth, the son of Joseph."

Philip was in full flow when he was interrupted. Thus far silence might mean consent and possibly did until Philip said the words *'Jesus of Nazareth, son of Joseph'"* Nathaniel's response was *'Nazareth! Can anything good come from there?'*

Perhaps there was religious prejudice in Nathaniel's mind. Bethlehem was mentioned in Old Testament prophecy in connection with the Messiah's birth—but there was no mention of Nazareth at all. This is only an opinion.

Philip's reply is the best one for dealing with someone who is prejudiced: *'Come and see (for yourself).'*

As in Simon, Jesus sees potential in Nathaniel and His greeting astonishes the man.

When Jesus saw Nathanael approaching, he said of him, "Here is a true Israelite, in whom there is no deceit." v.47

Nathaniel's response is natural and open. *"How do you know me?"* He asked. Jesus' answer is no less astonishing than before:

Jesus answered, "I saw you while you were still under the fig-tree before Philip called you." v. 48

Nathaniel was convinced. Hear his confession of faith.

Then Nathanael declared, "Rabbi, you are the Son of God; you are the King of Israel." v. 49

We see that Nathaniel had a well-stocked mind. So much of what Jesus said to him was reminiscent of Jacob in Genesis 28.12ff. This is confirmed for us by Jesus parting words. 1:50-51

Jesus said, "You believe because I told you I saw you under the fig-tree. You shall see greater things than that."
He then added, "Very truly I tell you, you shall see heaven open, and the angels of God ascending and descending on the Son of Man."

The converse between heaven and earth witnessed by the patriarch Jacob long ago will be re-enacted before Nathaniel's eyes. Indeed he will see greater things as the traffic between the two worlds attains it climax as Jesus' ministry moves to its conclusion.

Jesus, the Word of God made flesh,

is the new and supreme point

at which God and humanity intersect.

Thank You, Heavenly Father:

For the remarkable, faithful, preparatory ministry of John the Baptist making a way for the ministry of Jesus;

For the spiritual calibre of the first disciples, having first being disciples of John;

For the spirit of John the Baptist as he saw his disciples leave him to follow Jesus; it says so much about his integrity as the servant of Christ (John 3:30. *He must become greater; I must become less.*)

For Jesus' intimate knowledge of every one of us; and yet he is
prepared to trust us with the work of his kingdom;

For the fact that in Your love as the Father of Your Son, You
have placed everything in his hands. v. 35

In Jesus' Name, Amen

Chapter 2

John 2:1-12   **Jesus changes water into wine**

John 2:13-25   **Jesus clears the temple courts**

John 2:1-12

JESUS CHANGES WATER INTO WINE

The majority of weddings are happy occasions – unless something goes terribly wrong. This wedding in Cana had every indication that everything was in order. Then disaster happened: they had run out of wine!

> *On the third day a wedding took place at Cana in Galilee. Jesus' mother was there, ²and Jesus and his disciples had also been invited to the wedding. ³When the wine was gone, Jesus' mother said to him, 'They have no more wine. 2:1-3*

Sometimes I wonder where common sense goes when a wedding is being arranged. The most ordinary of humble people are determined to 'make a splash', or at least 'show off' a bit. Perhaps this couple had overstretched themselves.

In eastern culture the catering arrangements at a wedding were the responsibility of the groom's family; therefore family pride was 'at high water mark'. Well, on this day the wine ran out. Family feuds and court proceedings had been known to follow some weddings when this kind of thing happened. The shortage of wine could be interpreted as meanness on the part of the groom's family. They could be accused of being niggardly, and as having little respect for their guests. Mary, the mother of Jesus seemed to have been helping with catering and was among the first to be aware of the crisis that had arisen. She immediately turned to Jesus, as she had done many times down the years, and told him of the need.

Jesus believed in meeting people in the traffic lanes of life. Here he is a guest at a rural wedding. As he mingled with the other guests how many of them would have been aware of the uniqueness of the person they were meeting, sitting beside and talking to? The guests were in the presence of the incarnate Word, the Lamb of God and the King of Israel.

> [4]*'Woman, why do you involve me?' Jesus replied. 'My hour has not yet come.'*
> [5]*His mother said to the servants, 'Do whatever he tells you.'* 2:4-5

Jesus' response to his mother was not bad-mannered. It indicated that a change had come in their relationship. Previously it had been mother and son, ever since his birth. Now it was God the Word and a worshipper.

Mary seemed to get the point very quickly and in a few choice words she said to the servants, *'Do whatever he tells you.'* This smoothed the way for the waiters to do exactly as

Jesus directed them. It wasn't customary for a guest to have such a role.

What did Jesus do?

⁶Nearby stood six stone water jars, the kind used by the Jews for ceremonial washing, each holding from eighty to a hundred and twenty litres.
⁷Jesus said to the servants, 'Fill the jars with water'; so they filled them to the brim. 2:6-7

These jars were much bigger than the pitcher that a woman carried to the well when going to fetch water. The six jars would have had a total capacity of between 100 and 150 gallons of water. Jesus directed the servants to fill them and they filled them to the brim.

⁸Then he told them, 'Now draw some out and take it to the master of the banquet.' They did so. 2:8

What will the Master of Ceremonies have to say about the new wine? This connoisseur had never tasted wine like this before! He must enquire about its name and where it was obtained. He decided to ask the bridegroom.

⁹The master of the banquet tasted the water that had been turned into wine. He did not realise where it had come from, though the servants who had drawn the water knew. Then he called the bridegroom aside ¹⁰and said, 'Everyone brings out the choice wine first and then the cheaper wine after the guests have had too much to drink; but you have saved the best till now.' 2:9-10

This M.C. knew a few tricks about catering – such as serving wine of a poor quality when the guests already have had too much to drink!

This was the first time he had known wine of such excellent quality to be served last! Therefore he complimented the bridegroom.

Where do we go from here?

There can be no doubt that what Jesus provided was real wine. On the other hand we cannot judge the state of intoxication of the guests at this wedding. We simply do not know.

To construct a personal creed with regard to the consumption of alcoholic drinks (or abstinence from them) on the basis of this single occurrence in Ch. 2 would be inadequate.

Not only is there an ethical question to answer (the consumption of alcohol/alcoholic drinks) there is also a cultural question (as in France and other countries where wine is served with meals). You will not be surprised that Christians differ about the consumption of alcohol!

Are you an abstainer (a teetotaller)? Then follow your conviction, but do not enforce it on anyone else. You can advise but not compel. Do you sometimes drink alcohol? Remember to do it in moderation. Temperance in all things. Let everyone be fully persuaded in their own mind. If you are aware that a recovered or recovering alcoholic is part of your church or informal home group, you are doing them no favours by including alcohol on the menu.

What would you do in that instance?

The answer to this question is: we go where the *'sign'* takes us. John interprets the miracle in v. 11.

> *[11]What Jesus did here in Cana of Galilee was the first of the signs through which he revealed his glory; and his disciples believed in him.* 2:11

Recall 1:3 – 'through him all things were made'. What John recorded here is a miracle of creation wrought by the power of him who created all things.

John observed that the out-shining of his glory nourished the faith of his disciples. *'His disciples believed in him'* (Hence the title of this book.)

We might go further and say that 'the new wine' of the kingdom of God brought by Jesus contrasts with 'the old wine' of Judaism. This sign proclaims the direct presence and action of God in the world of nature and history.

Jesus changes the old wine of Judaism into the new wine of Christianity.

> *[12]After this he went down to Capernaum with his mother and brothers and his disciples. There they stayed for a few days.* 2:12

What a lovely touch with which to close this section of John 2. We can imagine Jesus and the disciples enjoying the attentions of his mother Mary.

Home, sweet home!

Thank You, Heavenly Father:

For the mutual respect between Jesus and his mother Mary; and for the way he helped her make the transfer from son/mother to believer/and Lord;

For how Jesus was able to enter into village life, without any compromising behaviour on his part.

For Jesus' masterful teaching skills and his complete knowledge of how ungodly people thought and behaved as they did; truly he knew what was in man.

In Jesus' Name, Amen

John 2:13-25

JESUS CLEARS THE TEMPLE COURTS.

A question arises here: why did John combine the two events in chapter 2, the changing of water into wine at Cana, and the cleansing of the temple? It has been suggested that these events are a pair of book-ends, one part that begins and another part that closes Jesus' ministry.

Bishop J. C. Ryle comments: 'To attend a marriage feast and to cleanse the temple were among the first events of our Lord's ministry at his first coming. To purify the visible church and hold a marriage supper will be among his first acts, when he comes again.'

> *After this he went down to Capernaum with his mother and brothers and his disciples. There they stayed for a few days. When it was almost time for the Jewish Passover, Jesus went up to Jerusalem.* 2:12-13

John mentions three Passovers in his gospel: 2:13; 6:4; 11:55ff. In the other gospels the cleansing of the Temple is recorded at the beginning of Passion Week (Matthew 21:12-17; Mark 11:15-18; Luke 19:45-46

After the wedding Jesus, together with his family and dis-ciples, went to Capernaum, a distance of about 18 miles as the crow flies. Following a short break at home, Jesus went to Jerusalem for the approaching Passover.

It is described as a *'Jewish'* Passover because it commemorated the deliverance of the people of Israel from Egyptian bondage (Exodus 12). It was a national festival.

John describes it as a *'Jewish'* festival which signifies that at the time of writing its observance was not regarded as a Christian obligation.

> *In the temple courts he found men selling cattle, sheep and doves, and others sitting at tables exchanging money.* 2:14

Jesus was distressed and grieved by what was happening in the Temple courts. He found the sacred place profaned by the extortionate practices of the animal-sellers and money-changers.

What was the issue here?

For Jesus the honour and glory of God are at stake: generally in the quality of the worship offered by the people, and specifically in their behaviour within the sacred precincts associated with the presence of God.

Burning with holy zeal, Jesus waded into the confusion of that religious marketplace and put an end (at least on this occasion) to the unholy business that was going on.

> *So he made a whip out of cords, and drove all from the temple courts, both sheep and cattle; he scattered the coins of the money-changers and overturned their tables. To those who sold doves he said, "Get these out of here! Stop turning my Father's house into a market!"* 2:15-16

We are left to imagine the impact of Jesus' actions. How did he escape the wrath of those whom he expelled from the place? Can we imagine the grievances he would have heard? There is no reason to think that the traders would take this treatment *'lying down'* – like submissive animals. Can't you hear their complaints?

'We have every right to be here!'

'We have been trading here for generations!'

'You've ruined our business!'

'You've bankrupted us! '

'You've taken the bread from our children's mouths!'

Jesus was not prepared to negotiate. His conviction was *'You should not have been here in the first place!' How dare you turn my Father's house into a market!"*

> *Then the Jews responded to him, "What miraculous sign can you show us to prove your authority to do all this?"* 2:18

Here is 'Official Israel' (representing the Temple authorities) come to deal with this upstart rabbi. They hadn't come to apologise to Him for their desecration of that holy place. No!

They were totally blind to what was happening before their eyes. The prophet Malachi had spoken of the events of this day.

> *"See, I will send my messenger, who will prepare the way before me. Then suddenly the Lord you are seeking will come to his temple; the messenger of the covenant, whom you desire, will come," says the LORD Almighty. But who can endure the day of his coming? Who can stand when he appears? For he will be like a refiner's fire or a launderer's soap. He will sit as a refiner and purifier of silver; he will purify the Levites and refine them like gold and silver. Then*

the LORD will have men who will bring offerings in righteousness,
Malachi 3:1-3

He would give them a sign all right—and did so then and there.

Jesus answered them, "Destroy this temple, and I will raise it again in three days." 2:19

He had set them a real puzzle!

The Jews replied, "It has taken forty-six years to build this temple, and you are going to raise it in three days?" 2:20

They were thoroughly confused—nor could they understand Jesus' words unless their minds were enlightened.

But the temple he had spoken of was his body. 2:21

And there, we may believe, the confrontation ended—for the moment. In John 2:22 the apostle inserted a note to show that the disciples also were wondering what exactly Jesus meant.

After he was raised from the dead, his disciples recalled what he had said. Then they believed the Scripture and the words that Jesus had spoken. 2:22

Before we leave this record of the cleansing of the temple at the beginning of Jesus' ministry, we need to meditate on the event and come to some conclusions about what the Holy Spirit is teaching here.

The whole incident was a confrontation between Jesus the incarnate Lord—and official Judaism.

Jesus predicted his death at the hands of the Jewish authorities, his burial and his glorious resurrection, the great sign that would authenticate his claims and this specific action (2:19).

Jesus is looking beyond the age of Temple worship, when it will have perished and its worship ceased, to the time when the worship of God everywhere will be inspired by the Holy Spirit and offered on the basis of the all-sufficient sacrifice of the Lamb of God.

Jesus is predicting nothing less that the reconstituting of the entire worship of God's people around his own person and mission.

Jesus' body, offered in sacrifice and raised in power, will be the new Temple where God and humanity, creator and creature, are reconciled.

Conclusion

Now while he was in Jerusalem at the Passover Feast, many people saw the miraculous signs he was doing and believed in his name. But Jesus would not entrust himself to them, for he knew all men. He did not need man's testimony about man, for he knew what was in a man. 2:23-25

Here is a tension that is always present whenever the facts about Jesus are presented to the minds of worldly men and women. Their definitions of *'faith'* and Jesus' definition of *'faith'* are two different things.

Many people saw the miraculous signs he was doing
and believed in his name.
But Jesus would not entrust himself to them.

Q. WHAT WAS THE BASIS OF THEIR 'BELIEVING IN HIS NAME'?

A. THEY SAW THE MIRACULOUS SIGNS HE WAS DOING.

What the people were calling **'faith'** was nothing more than a fascination with Jesus' miracles. Jesus defined **'faith'** as acceptance of him and reliance on him.

It's the difference between the faith of NATHANIEL (Ch. 1:47ff) and the faith of NICODEMUS (ch.3:1-2).

Compare the 'FAITH' of Nathaniel and the 'FAITH' of Nicodemus.

Nathaniel declared, 'Rabbi, you are the Son of God; you are the King of Israel.' Jesus said, 'You believe because I told you I saw you under the fig tree. You shall see greater things than that.' 1:49

NATHANIEL HAD TRUSTWORTHY FAITH.

He was honest and clear-sighted and had a remarkably clear grasp of who Jesus was.

JESUS ENTRUSTED HIMSELF TO NATHANIEL.

'Lit: *they trusted in his name, but Jesus did not entrust himself to them. 2:23-24*

There was a man of the Pharisees, named Nicodemus, a member of the Jewish ruling council. He came to Jesus by night and said, 'Rabbi, we know that you are a teacher come from God. For no one can do the miraculous signs you are doing if God were not with him. 3:1-2

<u>NICODEMUS HAD UNTRUSTWORTHY FAITH.</u>

His assessment of Jesus was based on the signs he had seen.

<u>JESUS DID NOT ENTRUST HIMSELF TO NICODEMUS.</u>

Thank You, Heavenly Father:

For the remarkable, faithful, preparatory ministry of John the Baptist making a way for the ministry of Jesus;

For the spiritual calibre of the first disciples, having first being disciples of John;

For the spirit of John the Baptist as he saw his disciples leave him to follow Jesus; it says so much about his integrity as the servant of Christ (John 3:30. *He must become greater; I must become less.*)

For Jesus' intimate knowledge of every one of us; and yet he is prepared to trust us with the work of his kingdom;

For his righteous anger when he saw the profanation of the Temple premises; when secularism came in, worship went out;

For the fact that in Your love as the Father of the Son, You have placed everything in his hands. John 3:35

In Jesus' Name, Amen.

Chapter 3

John 3:1-21   **Jesus teaches Nicodemus**

John 3:22-36   **John again testifies about Jesus**

John 3: 1–21

JESUS TEACHES NICODEMUS

Now there was a Pharisee, a man named Nicodemus who was a member of the Jewish ruling council. ²He came to Jesus at night and said, 'Rabbi, we know that you are a teacher who has come from God. For no one could perform the signs you are doing if God were not with him.' 3:1-2

Nicodemus may have been a learned man. We may presume that this was the case because of the position he held in the Sanhedrin, the highest Jewish Council of his day. I immediately want to add that he must have been a very simple-minded man because when he was on his way to have an interview with Jesus he was lining up a series of thoughts in his mind that would enable him to speak with Jesus on an equal footing. In fact he might well control the entire conversation. What presumption! What conceit!

A lot has been made of the fact that he came to see Jesus at night. We don't know his reason for doing this, therefore we will leave that as his business. However, for a few minutes let us listen and watch the meeting between Jesus and Nicodemus taking place. This is what is really important.

> *'Rabbi, we know that you are a teacher who has come from God. For no one could perform the signs you are doing if God were not with him.' 3:2*

The meeting is off to a good start because Nicodemus was most respectful in his opening remarks. So Nicodemus, a teacher in Israel, addresses another teacher. He discloses that in his estimation and that of his colleagues, 'we know' (i.e. we have come to the considered opinion / that as for your teaching and preaching and so on / and these signs that you are doing / we are convinced) that you have come from God. We have reached this position because no one could perform the signs you are doing if God were not with him.

Jesus took Nicodemus off the track on which he had planned for this discussion to run by the simple expedient of introducing a subject that neither Nicodemus nor his colleagues had ever considered, and about which they knew precisely nothing.

> *3Jesus replied, 'Very truly I tell you, no one can see the kingdom of God unless they are born again.' 3:3*

Nicodemus is out of his depth immediately. Two sentences have been spoken, and already Jesus has control of the conversation and Nicodemus is floundering, wondering how to respond to something he knows nothing about.

⁴ 'How can someone be born when they are old?' Nicodemus asked.
'Surely they cannot enter a second time into their mother's womb
to be born!' 3:4

The only births that Nicodemus had ever heard of or thought about were natural ones; but this teacher has a new line of thought on the subject. He is talking about being *'born again'*. While Nicodemus is still floundering. Jesus gives him some more information.

> *⁵Jesus answered, 'Very truly I tell you, no one can enter the kingdom*
> *of God unless they are born of water and the Spirit.'*
> *⁶Flesh gives birth to flesh, but the Spirit gives birth to spirit.*
> *⁷You should not be surprised at my saying, "You must be born*
> *again." 3:5-7*

Jesus had interviewed many an earnest seeker after God. But this man knows nothing about being *'born from above'*. Jesus explains to Nicodemus that there is natural birth and there is spiritual birth (vv. 6-7), and repeats the requirement of *'new birth'* for entering the kingdom of God (v. 8).

Then Jesus helps Nicodemus along another line of thought. 'Think of the wind' he says.

> *⁸The wind blows wherever it pleases. You hear its sound, but you*
> *cannot tell where it comes from or where it is going. So it is with*
> *everyone born of the Spirit.' 3:8*

Can't you hear Nicodemus heave a sigh?

> *⁹ 'How can this be?' Nicodemus asked.*

This conversation is wearing him out.

[10] 'You are Israel's teacher,' said Jesus, 'and do you not understand these things?' 3:10

Nicodemus' ignorance about spiritual birth lands him in total embarrassment. He is left without a word to say for himself.

In fact we may presume that shortly after this Jesus and Nicodemus parted company, because from here until the chapter's end it's difficult to tell where their conversation ends and John the apostle takes up the theme.

Perhaps the two were still together as far as John 3:21. If so, Nicodemus went away with his mind well-stirred, and thinking about the Old Testament narrative of the Serpent of Brass.

Nicodemus had commenced the conversation with the words *'we know' (v. 2)*. The *'we know'* of a ruler of the Jews was countered by the *'we know'* (vv. 11-12) of the Lord of Christian believers.

[11] 'Very truly I tell you, we speak of what we know, and we testify to what we have seen, but still you people do not accept our testimony [12]I have spoken to you of earthly things and you do not believe; how then will you believe if I speak of heavenly things? [13]No one has ever gone into heaven except the one who came from heaven– the Son of Man.' 3:11-13

Jesus admits that the things he was speaking about originated in heaven (not on earth).

I am from heaven and have come to tell you heavenly things, but your leaders do not believe me. (v. 11)

54

Is there any common ground on which these two will be in agreement?

Yes, both of them hold the Hebrew Scriptures in high regard. So Jesus speaks to Nicodemus about an Old Testament story from Israel's wanderings in the Wilderness in Moses' time.

Nicodemus, do you recall when the dying Israelites who had been bitten by serpents looked to the brass serpent that Moses held high, so that everyone could see it, and they were healed instantly? (Numbers 21)

Well, Nicodemus, listen to this: and Jesus shared the gospel application of this Old Testament narrative with him. These are new thoughts for this Jewish teacher.

> *[14]Just as Moses lifted up the snake in the wilderness, so the Son of Man must be lifted up, [15]that everyone who believes may have eternal life in him.'* 3:14-15

If Nicodemus will hear it, the application is clear: Jesus is saying that the Son of Man himself will be *'lifted up'* so that all who look trustingly to him will experience the 'new birth' and eternal life in the kingdom of God.

We don't know if vv.16ff were spoken by Jesus to Nicodemus or if John is taking up their theme to round off this very important chapter. Jesus had given Nicodemus plenty to think about and most importantly, had taken him to familiar scriptures that spoke about him.

Jesus had also given Nicodemus, in portable form, one of the greatest statements in all of the Bible, the very heart of the Gospel.

[16]For God so loved the world that he gave his one and only Son, that whoever believes in him shall not perish but have eternal life. [17]For God did not send his Son into the world to condemn the world, but to save the world through him. [18]Whoever believes in him is not condemned, but whoever does not believe stands condemned already because they have not believed in the name of God's one and only Son. 3:16-18

So we close the curtain on Nicodemus. We hope that he went away with his mind stretched thinking about God's view of mankind and his way of salvation.

After his brief encounter with Jesus Nicodemus went away knowing much more about Jesus and the new birth than many people in this country know today. How we long for a movement of the Holy Spirit opening people's eyes to understand God's plan of salvation. John's mind may have been running along this line also.

[19]This is the verdict: light has come into the world, but people loved darkness instead of light because their deeds were evil. [20]Everyone who does evil hates the light, and will not come into the light for fear that their deeds will be exposed. [21]But whoever lives by the truth comes into the light, so that it may be seen plainly that what they have done has been done in the sight of God. 3:19-21

If Nicodemus had left the scene, as we think he had, then perhaps John the apostle was still thinking about him. John was every inch an evangelist.

Perhaps on his way home he settled the matter one way or another. Did he accept what he had heard Jesus teach? Would he believe in Jesus, the Son of God from heaven, as his Saviour? We know that sometime later he became a secret disciple of

Jesus, but his Christian profession did not become public until he helped take the body of Jesus down from the cross.

Here is a commentary on Nicodemus and many like him.

The cardinal error of Nicodemus and his colleagues was the non-acceptance of the teaching of Jesus. *'You people still do not accept our testimony' (v. 11)*.

v. 17. Jesus had come into the world with a saving purpose.
[17]For God did not send his Son into the world to condemn the world, but to save the world through him.

v. 18. There is deliverance from condemnation.
[18]Whoever believes in him is not condemned, but whoever does not believe stands condemned already because they have not believed in the name of God's one and only Son.

v. 19. Why do people remain in unbelief?
[19]This is the verdict: light has come into the world, but people loved darkness instead of light because their deeds were evil.

vv. 20-21 The response of people to gospel light reveals their character.
[20]Everyone who does evil hates the light, and will not come into the light for fear that their deeds will be exposed. [21]But whoever lives by the truth comes into the light, so that it may be seen plainly that what they have done has been done in the sight of God. 3:17-21

Thank You, Heavenly Father:

For John's diligence in recording the interview between Jesus and Nicodemus; to this day the help and assurance we receive from it are beyond calculation

For the fact that in times past you spoke to the leaders of Israel through the prophets, but in these last days You have spoken to us in Your Son.

For John chapter 3 and verse 16, 'the gospel in a nutshell', which many of us learned in childhood. We are still exploring its meaning and living in its assurance.

For the Old Testament Bible stories that look forward to the Cross and Death of Jesus: such as the serpent in the wilderness etc;

In Jesus Name, Amen.

John 3:22–36

JOHN AGAIN TESTIFIES ABOUT JESUS

²²After this, Jesus and his disciples went out into the Judean countryside, where he spent some time with them, and baptised. 3:22

Clearly John is following Jesus' public ministry. It took Jesus to the Judean countryside. People became believers in him and were baptised without delay. John's continuing ministry took him to Aenon, near Salim where his ministry was again in full swing.

²³Now John also was baptising at Aenon near Salim, because there was plenty of water, and people were coming and being baptised. ²⁴(This was before John was put in prison.) 3:23-24

This seemed somewhat mysterious to people who had seen John baptising people before Jesus' public ministry began and so they came to John with a query.

²⁵An argument developed between some of John's disciples and a certain Jew over the matter of ceremonial washing. ²⁶They came to John and said to him, 'Rabbi that man who was with you on the other side of the Jordan – the one you testified about – look, he is baptising, and everyone is going to him.' 3:25-26

They were possibly surprised to find not the slightest trace of jealousy in John the Baptist because Jesus had many people coming to him, repenting of their sins and seeking baptism. John had several sound principles in mind. This was because John understood his work in relation to the ministry of Jesus.

> *[27]To this John replied, 'A person can receive only what is given them from heaven. [28]You yourselves can testify that I said, "I am not the Messiah but am sent ahead of him."*
> *[29]The bride belongs to the bridegroom. The friend who attends the bridegroom waits and listens for him, and is full of joy when he hears the bridegroom's voice. That joy is mine, and it is now complete.*
> *[30]He must become greater; I must become less.'*3:27-30

Nothing could give John the Baptist greater pleasure and fulfilment than to see people coming to Jesus and professing faith in him. John was like a best man and Jesus was like a bridegroom (v. 29). John was looking after the bridegroom's interests and considered himself well rewarded.

Please don't miss John's principles of Christian service in John 1:27 & 30. They are golden words and I know that many of God's servants in after years didn't hesitate to borrow them.

Footnote: John 3:31-36

John did not write his gospel in chapters. However, it is clear that he had an orderly mind. He may have viewed the previous paragraphs (30 verses in our Bibles) as relating to Nicodemus, and was already thinking ahead to writing some major paragraphs about Jesus and the disciples taking the gospel to the Samaritans (chapter 4 in our Bibles). If there is any weight in my suggestion it seems that he took the opportunity to round off the Nicodemus section with an outline of important gospel truths (verses 31-36 in our Bibles). They seem to have as their subject:

'The consequences of accepting and rejecting the Son of God.'

[31]The one who comes from above is above all; the one who is from the earth belongs to the earth, and speaks as one from the earth. The one who comes from heaven is above all. 3:31

John had Jesus in mind when he wrote the above words. He is God's supreme spokesman. None other speaks with the authority of Jesus.

[32]He testifies to what he has seen and heard, but no one accepts his testimony. [33]Whoever has accepted it has certified that God is truthful.
[34]For the one whom God has sent speaks the words of God, for God gives the Spirit without limit. [35]The Father loves the Son and has placed everything in his hands. 3:32-35

John is testifying here that Jesus has revealed everything that mankind needs to know about God but his testimony has been rejected (v. 32). Acceptance of that revelation is a testimony to God's truthfulness. v. 33.

Jesus, as God's spokesman is marked by integrity in everything he speaks because God has given him the Spirit without limit. v. 34.

The Father loves the Son, and has placed everything in his hands. v. 35.

[36]Whoever believes in the Son has eternal life, but whoever rejects the Son will not see life, for God's wrath remains on them.
Whoever believes in the Son: has eternal life,
Whoever rejects the Son: will not see life,
for God's wrath remains on him. 3:36

Thank You, Heavenly Father:

For the Old Testament Bible stories that look forward to the Cross and Death of Jesus: such as the serpent in the wilderness etc;

For the secret, silent ministry of the Holy Spirit who opens the minds of sinners, reveals their sinfulness and then points them to Jesus as their only Saviour;

For the fact that whoever believes in the Son has eternal life.

For every preacher and evangelist, who like so many John the Baptists are preparing the way for Jesus to enter many hearts.

In Jesus' Name, Amen

Chapter 4

John 4:1-26

JESUS TALKS WITH A SAMARITAN WOMAN

J esus was not a professional preacher – confined to a pulpit or a building. He was a *'people-person'*, hugely and genuinely interested in the lives and interests of ordinary folk. This is why he was so good at initiating conversations with total strangers.

Pastors need to be *'people orientated'* at all times ever thinking and praying about the circumstances and spiritual needs of their congregations. The communication process involves relationships.

John continues to document how various kinds and classes of people were reached by Jesus and came to believe in him as the Son of God.

The Pharisees heard that Jesus was gaining and baptising more disciples than John, although in fact it was not Jesus who baptised, but his disciples. When the Lord learned of this, he left Judea and went back once more to Galilee. Now he had to go through Samaria. 4:1-4

When chapter 4 opens John is explaining why Jesus moved his ministry to a new location. He had two reasons for doing this. Firstly, Jesus was aware that the Pharisees were commenting unfavourably about the results of his ministry compared to those of John the Baptist, because Jesus was gaining and baptising more disciples than John. Competitiveness had no place in Jesus' methods in the work of God, therefore he moved his preaching mission north to Galilee. Secondly, there was a woman in Samaria that he purposed to meet. There was an alternative route he could have taken, but he chose to go *through* Samaria. It wasn't a geographical necessity, but an evangelistic one.

> *Now he had to go through Samaria. So he came to a town in Samaria called Sychar, near the plot of ground Jacob had given to his son Joseph. Jacob's well was there, and Jesus, tired as he was from the journey, sat down by the well. It was about the sixth hour.* 4:4-6

Memories of the Old Testament come to mind with the mention of Sychar and Jacob and Joseph. *'Jacob's Well'*, as it was known locally had become a landmark for travellers.

Here is a truly pastoral scene. We can imagine the well, possibly shaded with a few trees. We can share the weariness of Jesus, because we have often been tired when travelling. We note that it was about the sixth hour, which by Roman reckoning was noon, when the sun was high in the heavens.

The scene also brings before us the reality of Jesus' physical nature, a doctrine that is beautifully encapsulated in John 1:14 *'The Word became flesh and dwelt among us.'*

When a Samaritan woman came to draw water, Jesus said to her, "Will you give me a drink?" 4:7-8

Jesus shocked her by speaking to her at all! Women didn't have a high place in either Jewish or Samaritan society, and for a man who wasn't her husband or a relative to speak to a woman just wasn't done.

The rabbis had ruled: *'One should not talk with a woman on the street, and certainly not with someone else's wife, because of the gossip of men,'* and *'It is forbidden to give a woman any greeting.'*

Jesus' simple request that she give him a drink of water was a natural and tactful opening to their conversation. They shared a common need for water.

The Samaritan woman said to him, "You are a Jew and I am a Samaritan woman. How can you ask me for a drink?" (For Jews do not associate with Samaritans.) 4:9

Whether by his language or dress the woman quickly perceived that she was speaking to a Jew. She responded instinctively; her cultural background told her that this shouldn't be happening. Jews didn't *'share vessels'* with the Samaritans. The hatred between them was intense.

(The sentence in brackets is John's historical note.)

The division reached back through the centuries to the division of the kingdom of Israel after the death of King Solomon. The Samaritans were 'the survivors' of the old northern kingdom of Israel. They had a separate temple on Mt. Gerizim, and their scriptures were confined to the five books of Moses (the Pentateuch).

> *Jesus answered her, "If you knew the gift of God and who it is that asks you for a drink, you would have asked him and he would have given you living water." 4:10*

It is now clear that Jesus' opening words were his initiative to open a conversation and share with this woman the truth about *'living water'*. He had spoken to Nicodemus about *'the new birth'*; to this woman he spoke about *'living water'*.

Jesus' words had aroused her interest, so, setting aside any prejudice she might have had towards Jews, she pursues the conversation.

> *"Sir,"* the woman said, *"You have nothing to draw with and the well is deep. Where can you get this living water? Are you greater than our father Jacob, who gave us the well and drank from it himself, as did also his sons and his flocks and herds?" 4:11-12*

She is still thinking about the water in the well. *'Living water'* is an entirely new concept to her. However, she has just confessed Jacob as her spiritual father.

> *Jesus answered, "Everyone who drinks this water will be thirsty again, but whoever drinks the water I give him will never thirst. Indeed, the water I give him will become in him a spring of water welling up to eternal life." 4:13-14*

Now Jesus adds another strand to his teaching: The water in the well is spring water, but isn't living water. *'The water I'm talking about isn't in the well.'*

We wonder did she hear Jesus say: *the water I give him will become in him a spring of water welling up to eternal life."*

> *The woman said to him, "Sir, give me this water so that I won't get thirsty and have to keep coming here to draw water." 4:15*

She is fascinated more with cutting down on her daily chores than she is in this gift of eternal life. Any inhibitions she may have had about talking to this Jew have gone. She is speaking freely.

> *He told her, "Go, call your husband and come back." 4:16*

This was a further shock to her system. She found herself not protesting, or covering her past, or inventing an alibi, but answering candidly.

> *"I have no husband," she replied.*
> *Jesus said to her, "You are right when you say you have no husband. The fact is, you have had five husbands, and the man you now have is not your husband. What you have just said is quite true." 4:17-18*

She was shocked by Jesus' knowledge of her personal life. After five marriages, she is now living in a common-law marriage (which the Jews did not recognise): hence her answer: 'I have no husband'. Where will the conversation go from here?

> *"Sir," the woman said, "I can see that you are a prophet. Our fathers worshipped on this mountain, but you Jews claim that the place where we must worship is in Jerusalem."*

Her conversation has moved to another level – she is now talking about worshipping God. She knows the Samaritan way. She knows that the Jews worship differently at Jerusalem. (What is a woman like me to do in all this religious confusion?) *She has a fixation with the place of worship.* 4:19-20

Jesus taught her some things she did not know.

> *Jesus declared, "Believe me, woman, a time is coming when you will worship the Father neither on this mountain nor in Jerusalem. You Samaritans worship what you do not know; we worship what we do know, for salvation is from the Jews.*
> *Yet a time is coming and has now come when the true worshippers will worship the Father in spirit and truth, for they are the kind of worshippers the Father seeks.*
> *God is spirit, and his worshippers must worship in spirit and in truth." 4:21-24*

She did not know who to worship, where to worship or how to worship.

Jesus affirmed that the Samaritans were worshipping ignorantly (v. 22), but did not stop there. He went on to say that salvation is from the Jews: e.g. the witness of the OT and the incarnation of the Eternal Word among men.

She had to learn that God is a spirit, and must be worshipped in spirit and in truth.

She responded with the only certainty that she possessed

> *The woman said, "I know that Messiah" (called Christ) "is coming. When he comes, he will explain everything to us." 4:25*

Jesus shocked the woman by telling her that she was speaking to the Messiah in person.

Then Jesus declared, "I who speak to you am he." 4:26

At this point the woman accepted Jesus by faith, having a clear knowledge of who he was.

John 4:27-42

MANY SAMARITANS BELIEVE

INTERRUPTION:
The disciples return from their shopping expedition.

27Just then his disciples returned and were surprised to find him talking with a woman. But no one asked, 'What do you want?' or 'Why are you talking with her?' 4:27

The disciples are surprised that Jesus had ignored the age-old taboo about a man speaking to a woman! Jesus did not allow anything to stand in the way of his evangelistic initiatives. Perhaps we attach too much importance to social mōres and allow barriers to get in the way of our personal witness for Jesus. I found the application of this verse to myself very powerful indeed. Social and sexual conventions had become ingrained in them and had taken the edge off their evangelism. If we had opportunity to question them what would they have to say for themselves?

THE STORY CONTINUES

28Then, leaving her water jar, the woman went back to the town and said to the people, 29'Come, see a man who told me everything I've ever done. Could this be the Messiah?' 30They came out of the town and made their way towards him. 4:28-30

In her excitement and enthusiasm the woman forgets about her water pot. She doesn't know a single word of evangelical jargon. It's refreshing to hear her talking about Jesus in her own words: *'Come, see a man who told me everything I've ever done. Could this be the Messiah?'*

There are no more zealous, attractive evangelists than those who have newly followed Jesus. Perhaps she had been an unpopular figure in her town due to her questionable character; but she had caught the attention of the local people who came to investigate and see Jesus for themselves.

INTERRUPTION

The disciples are concerned about Jesus having some food.

> [31]*Meanwhile his disciples urged him, 'Rabbi, eat something.'* [32]*But he said to them, 'I have food to eat that you know nothing about.'* [33]*Then his disciples said to each other, 'Could someone have brought him food?'* 4:31-33

Jesus hadn't thought about food during the disciples' absence. For him the service of the kingdom sustained and fulfilled him. The mild rebuke was intended to teach them a lesson; leading the woman to salvation was his nourishment. We know that the disciples could be so dull at times! They missed his point entirely and showed it when they asked: 'Could someone have brought him food?' Jesus cleared up their difficulty.

> [34] *'My food,' said Jesus, 'is to do the will of him who sent me and to finish his work.* 4:34

The woman had difficulty understanding 'living water'. Here the disciples cannot understand 'his food'. Doing the will of God is Jesus' food and is such for his followers also.

Jesus used a colloquialism or proverbial saying to awaken the disciples to their present evangelistic opportunities. They needed to be up and doing the Lord's work.

> *[35]Don't you have a saying, "It's still four months until harvest"? I tell you, open your eyes and look at the fields! They are ripe for harvest. 4: 35*

If they will follow Jesus' pointing finger they would see hundreds of Samaritans (probably wearing white clothing) coming their way – a gospel harvest field if ever there was one!

> *[36]Even now the one who reaps draws a wage and harvests a crop for eternal life, so that the sower and the reaper may be glad together. [37]Thus the saying "One sows and another reaps" is true. [38]I sent you to reap what you have not worked for. Others have done the hard work, and you have reaped the benefits of their labour.'*
> 4:36-38

Verse 38 shows that others had sown the gospel seed in Samaria – their identity is not disclosed. Their initial work was hardest. Now the disciples are privileged to enter into their labours.

Sowers and reapers make a wonderful partnership in harvest. We need to work together at all times so that the church can reach the world.

> *[39]Many of the Samaritans from that town believed in him because of the woman's testimony, 'He told me everything I've ever done.'4:39*

Was their faith *'saving faith'* that rested entirely in the person of Jesus? I think we are about to find out.

[40]So when the Samaritans came to him, they urged him to stay with them, and he stayed two days. [41]And because of his words many more became believers. 4:40-41

There is no doubt that this response to the gospel was Christ-centred. So excited were the Samaritans that they begged Jesus to stay with them; and he stayed two days. We are left to imagine the conversations that took place and teaching opportunities Jesus used to establish these new believers in the Word of God.

[42]They said to the woman, 'We no longer believe just because of what you said; now we have heard for ourselves, and we know that this man really is the Saviour of the world.' 4:42

The name that the Samaritans gave Jesus was significant. For generations they had been told that they were shut out from God's mercy. But now the excluded are the included and their confidence that he had accepted them inspired this wonderful Name: the Saviour of the World.

Personal contact with Christ makes faith complete.

Thank You, Heavenly Father:

For Your superintendence of a spiritual conversation that is
    taking place amid a chaos of constant interruption;
For all of us who, like the Samaritan woman, met Jesus one day
    in a quiet place, and there a transaction took place between
    us that sealed our eternal destiny;

For the Samaritan women's eagerness to witness to her contemporaries about Jesus;

For Your guidance every day leading us to people who want someone to tell them about how to know Jesus.

In Jesus' Name, Amen.

JOHN 4: 43-54

JESUS HEALS AN OFFICIAL'S SON

⁴³After the two days he left for Galilee. ⁴⁴(Now Jesus himself had pointed out that a prophet has no honour in his own country.) ⁴⁵When he arrived in Galilee, the Galileans welcomed him. They had seen all that he had done in Jerusalem at the Passover Festival, for they also had been there. 4:43

It must have been difficult for the Samaritan believers to bid farewell to their new-found Messiah and Saviour. On Jesus' part he was walking in harmony with heaven and so his steps turned towards Galilee.

This visit to Galilee was a 'home-coming'–and we are told by John that Jesus quoted a proverb: 'a prophet has no honour in his own country'. The other gospels quote Jesus on this–but in various situations.

Does Jesus mean by 'his own country' the Judea he was leaving in which he had been born or the Galilee to which he was going where he had grown up? His words could apply to both places.

In the course of his ministry Jesus was never really identified with Judea but became known as the prophet from Galilee. When entering Jerusalem on Palm Sunday (Matt. 21:11) he was hailed by the crowds with the words: *'This is the prophet from Nazareth in Galilee.'*

The people of Galilee welcomed him, apparently contradicting the proverb.

[45]When he arrived in Galilee, the Galileans welcomed him. They had seen all that he had done in Jerusalem at the Passover Festival, for they also had been there. 4:43

What motivated their faith? John seems to be warning us that the Galileans had 'faulty faith' – like Nicodemus in Ch. 3:2.

These Galileans had been in Jerusalem for the Passover and had witnessed Jesus cleansing the temple (Ch. 2:12-15) and had been mightily impressed. That was all.

The proverb was still applicable – the welcome of the Galileans did not represent saving faith in Jesus.

A return visit to Cana, the site of his first miracle, gave Jesus opportunity to do more mighty works.

Jesus met a royal official who urgently needed his help. The man had a very sick son lying at home in Capernaum. The boy was dying.

[46]Once more he visited Cana in Galilee, where he had turned the water into wine. And there was a certain royal official whose son lay ill at Capernaum. [47]When this man heard that Jesus had arrived in Galilee from Judea, he went to him and begged him to come and heal his son, who was close to death. 4:46-47

The man believed that Jesus could heal his boy, and leaving the boy at home, had undertaken the long journey (there and back) of about 40 miles, to ask Jesus to come to his house. Jesus' reply seems harsh to our ears.

[48] 'Unless you people see signs and wonders,' Jesus told him, 'you will never believe.' 4:48

Faith that needed miraculous signs and wonders was fragile faith, it was faith that needed a crutch. It was the kind of faith to which Jesus did not commit himself. He said this for the sake of the Galileans – and for the official whose faith in Jesus' ability required his physical presence in Capernaum.

The official responded with a most urgent and heartfelt plea:

[49]The royal official said, 'Sir, come down before my child dies.'
[50] 'Go,' Jesus replied, 'your son will live.'
The man took Jesus at his word and departed. 4:49-50

The official's journey may have required an overnight stop. He met some of his servants coming looking for him with very good news.

[51]While he was still on the way, his servants met him with the news that his boy was living. [52]When he enquired as to the time when his son got better, they said to him, 'Yesterday, at one in the afternoon, the fever left him.'
[53]Then the father realised that this was the exact time at which Jesus had said to him, 'Your son will live.' So he and his whole household believed. 4:51-53

The respect of this man for Jesus and the confidence with which he came to him are exemplary.

[54]This was the second sign Jesus performed after coming from Judea to Galilee. 4:54

Thank You, Heavenly Father:

We thank You that the 'new birth' means being 'born from above' and is the work of the Holy Spirit shining gospel light into our souls, so that we are brought out of darkness and into marvellous light;

We thank you also for how the Holy Spirit can penetrate barriers of unbelief in sinners' minds and hearts so that even the most unlikely people become believers in Jesus;

That the kingdom of God is open to people of all nationalities, all religions and cultures; this is clearly demonstrated in the gospels and we know it is true and is happening wherever the gospel goes;

That whatever occupied us in our unsaved days the Holy Spirit taught us many things even before we knew Jesus as Saviour; in some cases a highly developed conscience of right and wrong.

In Jesus' Name. Amen.

Chapter 5

John 5:1-15	Healing At the pool of Bethesda
John 5:16-30	The authority of the Son
John 5:31-47	Testimonies about Jesus

John 5:1-15

THE THIRD SIGN: HEALING AT THE POOL OF BETHESDA

According to John there were four Passovers in the three and a half years of Jesus' ministry (2:13; 5:1; 6:4 & 11:55). This was the second one – the first being the occasion on which he cleansed the Temple (2:12-22).

> *Some time later, Jesus went up to Jerusalem for one of the Jewish festivals.*
> *Now there is in Jerusalem near the Sheep Gate a pool, which in Aramaic is called Bethesda and which is surrounded by five covered colonnades. 5:1-2*

Archaeologists have uncovered the site in the north quarter of Jerusalem, thus confirming the location of John's narrative.

Bible translators face a difficulty in vv. 3 & 4 because manuscript evidence is poor. The KJV supplies the verses – others provide a footnote.

> *For an angel went down at a certain season into the pool, and troubled the water: whosoever then first after the troubling of the water stepped in was made whole of whatsoever disease he had.* 5:4 (KJV)

The translators' footnote tells us why so many disabled people came to the pool. The pool had spa-like healing properties. It was said that an angel stirred the water at certain times and the first person into the water received some physical benefit.

> *One who was there had been an invalid for thirty-eight years. When Jesus saw him lying there and learned that he had been in this condition for a long time, he asked him, "Do you want to get well?"* 5:5-6

One man who was there had been an invalid for 38 years, without any improvement in his condition. Jesus enquired about the man and learned that *'he had been in this condition for a long time.'* He asked the man a leading question: *'Do you want to get well?'*

There is more in this question than meets the eye.

One commentator says *'An eastern beggar often loses a good living by being cured'*. It's possible that this man's whole life had been built around his handicap.

What was Jesus' reason for coming to the Pool that day?

Why did he single out this man from among so many others? Why heal him, and not everyone who was there? We can only say that in this case, as in all cases, God's gifts are grace gifts.

"Sir," the invalid replied, "I have no-one to help me into the pool when the water is stirred. While I am trying to get in, someone else goes down ahead of me." 5:7

The way the man answered Jesus' question is revealing.

He didn't answer the question with a direct *'Yes'* or *'No'* – but rather talked about his double-handicap. In addition to his invalidity he had the problem that other people could get into the water before him. So did

'Get up! Pick up your mat and walk.' Jesus' bidding carried healing and enabling power: The man was cured instantly and picked up his mat and walked. After 38 years' of handicap Jesus gave this man wholeness of body and life.

Then Jesus said to him, "Get up! Pick up your mat and walk." At once the man was cured; he picked up his mat and walked. The day on which this took place was a Sabbath, 5:8-9

The verb for 'get up' will be used again in the following dialogue for the life-giving effect of Jesus' call at the last day. 5: 28-29

The healing had been done on the Sabbath day and immediately *'official Israel'* pounced on the man for breaking the law of the Sabbath by carrying his mat. In fact, he had not broken the Sabbath law of Exodus 20:8-11 at all.

At once the man was cured; he picked up his mat and walked. The day on which this took place was a Sabbath, and so the Jewish leaders said to the man who had been healed, "It is the Sabbath; the law forbids you to carry your mat." 5:9-10

The Jews seemed to major on the Sabbath Law because they saw it as a protection against paganism. However with them the *letter* of the law had replaced its *spirit*.

They did not see that they had put themselves and all others in bondage by their use of the Sabbath law. When they confronted the man they expressed neither wonder at his healing nor any interest in his new life with all its implications for his future. The man's answer to their question was their opportunity to follow it up: *'The man who made me well said to me, 'Pick up your mat and walk.'*

> *But he replied, "The man who made me well said to me, 'Pick up your mat and walk.' "So they asked him, "Who is this fellow who told you to pick it up and walk?" The man who was healed had no idea who it was, for Jesus had slipped away into the crowd that was there. 5:11-13*

The best they could do was to answer scathingly: *"Who is this fellow who told you to pick it up and walk?"*

The man didn't know the name of his healer because Jesus had slipped away. We will not fault the man for his ignorance of Jesus' identity. In this regard there are so many like him in our world today.

> *Later Jesus found him at the temple and said to him, "See, you are well again. Stop sinning or something worse may happen to you." The man went away and told the Jews that it was Jesus who had made him well. 5:14-15*

The Jews had treated the man with contempt.

It is thrilling to see, by contrast, that later Jesus found him.

He had an assurance for him and also a warning. *'See you are well again. Stop sinning or something worse may happen to you.'*

There was something in this man's life that Jesus knew about—hence the warning. His physical healing had not been followed by spiritual healing. We would like to know if this greater, spiritual healing took place later.

Jesus' words to him warn him of the need to respond to the grace of God in his life by repenting of his sin lest he face a worse fate. The something worse was probably the coming last judgment.

The man seems to have been blind to the malice of the Jews toward Jesus because he went to them and identified Jesus as his healer.

The Jews used the ministry of Jesus on the Sabbath day to launch an attack on him, *the Jews persecuted him.* John 5:16

Thank You, Heavenly Father:

For the genuineness of the miracle that Jesus performed on this crippled man; he was able to pick up his mat and walk immediately on Jesus' bidding him to do so; we share his gratitude;

For the fact that Jesus did not allow the sabbatarianism of the Jews to hinder the transformation of this man's life;

That both Jesus and his Father can work every day without the hindrance of man-made Sabbath rules;

In Jesus' Name, Amen.

John 5: 16-30
THE AUTHORITY OF THE SON

Who are the people whom John called 'the Jews'?

H e is not referring to the common people, who belonged to the Jewish faith, but to their leaders i.e. *'the chief priests, the elders and the scribes'* who dogged Jesus' footsteps all the way to the cross.

They were 'the religious police of Judaism'.

Had Jesus ignored them our Bibles would lack John 5:16-30 – an important part of what has been called the key chapter of the Gospel of John.

Why is that? Because this section of the chapter contains the strongest proofs for the Deity of Jesus Christ.

Had Jesus ignored his persecutors and walked away from the scene of the miracle, an opportunity to look them in the eye and speak to them in the strongest possible terms about His Divine Sonship would have been lost.

They had accused Him of claiming to be equal with God'

Well, let them hear the evidence from His own lips as He makes no less than three substantial claims, indicating three prerogatives in which He is most certainly equal with God.

Jesus is equal with God in HIS NATURE vv. 17-18

[17]In his defence Jesus said to them, "My Father is always at his work to this very day, and I, too, am working." [18]For this reason the Jews tried all the more to kill him; not only was he breaking the Sabbath, but he was even calling God his own Father, making himself equal with God. 5:17-18

Jesus had a unique relationship with God: God was His Father. V. 18 is one of the strongest statements of Christ's deity, and it comes as an accusation from His enemies.

As the son of a man has the nature of man, so the Son of God has the nature of God. God didn't stop for Sabbath rests in the course of His work, neither does Jesus His Son. Neither God the Father nor God the Son needs to rest on the Sabbath day from their work. Read v. 17 again:

"My Father is always at his work to this very day, and I, too, am working."

Both are free to work on the Sabbath without having to put up with the criticisms of self-righteous men.

Jesus is equal with God in HIS POWER vv. 19-21

Jesus gave them this answer: "Very truly I tell you, the Son can do nothing by himself; he can do only what he sees his Father doing, because whatever the Father does the Son also does. 5:19

The Jews – and the general public – had witnessed a miracle of healing performed by Jesus. What was the explanation for it?

Jesus explained that nothing He did was on his own initiative or by his own power; the miracle occurred because Jesus did what he saw His Father doing.

Jesus gave a reason for this harmonious working between God the Father and God the Son. It was because of the love of the Father for his Son: that the Son also shared the power of God.

For the Father loves the Son and shows him all he does. Yes, to your amazement he will show him even greater things than these. 5:20

Jesus was equal with the Father because both had the power to give life.

This was clarified in the course of his ministry. Jesus would reveal himself as -

the Bread of Life (6:33-35);

the Light that gives Life (8.12 & 9.5);

the Door to Abundant Life (10:9);

the Shepherd who gives His life for the Sheep (10.11);

the Resurrection and the Life (11:25);

the Way, the Truth and the Life (14:6);

and the Vine that gives the branches life (15:5).

For just as the Father raises the dead and gives them life, even so the Son gives life to whom he is pleased to give it. 5:21

In the course of his ministry Jesus would give physical life to Lazarus (11:41-44); to a ruler's daughter (Matt 9:18ff), and to a Widow's Son in a town called Nain (Luke 7:17ff).

Jesus is equal with God in HIS NATURE

Jesus is equal with God in HIS POWER

Jesus is equal with God in HIS JUDGMENT vv. 22-24

22Moreover, the Father judges no-one, but has entrusted all judgment to the Son, 23that all may honour the Son just as they honour the Father.

Whoever does not honour the Son does not honour the Father, who sent him.

24"Very truly I tell you, whoever hears my word and believes him who sent me has eternal life and will not be condemned; he has crossed over from death to life. 5:22-24

In v. 22a Jesus made a very big statement:

The Father has already made the commitment to leave the execution of judgment in the hands of the Son.

In v. 22b he made a further major statement:

The consequence of this equality is that the Son is worthy of the same worship that is due to the Father.

So here is a further annoyance to the *'Jewish Religious Police'* – but what is annoyance to them is a joy for all who know who the Son of God is. Here Jesus is calling on people to worship Him with the same honour they would have toward the Father.

It is the will of the Father that His Son Jesus Christ should have the preeminence in all things.

To hear and receive the word of Jesus Christ as the Word of God, is to pass from condemnation into eternal life. Has this experience been yours?

Q. What is the authority that has been committed to Jesus Christ the Son of God?

A. Three prerogatives of God are in the hands of Jesus Christ.

ALL LIFE IS IN HIS HANDS. vv. 25-26

Very truly I tell you, a time is coming and has now come when the dead will hear the voice of the Son of God and those who hear will live. For as the Father has life in himself, so he has granted the Son to have life in himself. 5:25-26

Jesus' authority to bring the dead to life is two-fold. It includes restoration to wholeness of life (as in the case of the man healed at Bethesda) and the bestowal of eternal life – as in v. 24 – He alone has the words of eternal life.

ALL JUDGMENT IS IN HIS HANDS. v. 27

And he has given him authority to judge because he is the Son of Man. 5:27

Jesus is uniquely qualified to be the judge of mankind.

First of all He is the Son of God, who by his incarnation became the Son of Man. 5:27

He came into the world to save sinners. It is part of his identity that He is also the judge of mankind. His very presence in the world is a judgment on all that is evil and false. Jesus has exclusive and ultimate authority over every person on earth. *The Father has entrusted all judgment to the Son.*

Secondly He knew what was in man. 2:24-25

He knew the thoughts of men, the depravity of the human heart. He was rejected by men and received their foulest blasphemies. He suffered at the hands of men. He knew the nature of those among whom He lived, those whom he had come to seek and to save.

There is justice in the fact that the one who died to be our Saviour is also our Judge.

Thirdly, the sins of the world were laid on Him at the Cross.

But he was pierced for our transgressions, he was crushed for our iniquities; the punishment that brought us peace was upon him, and by his wounds we are healed.

We all, like sheep, have gone astray, each of us has turned to his own way; and the LORD has laid on him the iniquity of us all. Isaiah 53:5-6

The Holy Spirit enabled Isaiah to state these facts of salvation so plainly and personally.

All judgment is in His hands.

All life is in his hands

All judgment is in his hands.

ALL RESURRECTION IS IN HIS HANDS. vv. 28-29

"Do not be amazed at this, for a time is coming when all who are in their graves will hear his voice and come out—those who have done good will rise to live, and those who have done evil will rise to be condemned. 5:28-29

For years I have believed that Jesus meant these words to be understood in a straight-forward and evangelical sense and that is how I will handle them now.

Just as Jesus commanded the paralytic at the pool of Bethesda with the words ''Pick up your mat and walk" so the day will dawn on which He will say to all who are in the graves 'GET UP!' and 'COME OUT!' and there will be instant obedience.

Those who have done well will rise to life, and those who have done evil will rise to be condemned.

These are the facts as we have received them!
ALL LIFE IS IN HIS HANDS
ALL JUDGMENT IS IN HIS HANDS.
ALL RESURRECTION IS IN HIS HANDS.
In v. 30 Jesus repeats the themes of v. 19
and ties the section (16-30) together.
All Jesus does: speaking, giving life and judging-
comes from his Father and reveals the Father.

By myself I can do nothing; I judge only as I hear, and my judgment is just, for I seek not to please myself but him who sent me. 5:30

Thank You, Heavenly Father:

We know that our Lord Jesus Christ was under intense pressure when he delivered the great claims and statements of this section of the Scriptures; we thank You for the assurance and hope his words minister to us as we read them at this late stage of history, and we bring You our joyful worship; For all who have eternal life through faith in Jesus Christ their Lord and Saviour;

'*We praise Thee, O God, for the Son of Thy love, for Jesus, who died and is now gone above.*' (Another hymn learned in childhood. JRG)

In Jesus' Name, Amen.

John 5: 31-47

TESTIMONIES ABOUT JESUS

J esus is referring to a principle enshrined in the Law of Moses: Every man's testimony must be corroborated by at least two witnesses.

"If I testify about myself, my testimony is not valid.' 5:31

Jesus is not confessing that his solitary testimony is false. He is saying that his witness alone is not enough, because the Jews would simply not accept it.

Under Jewish, Roman and Greek law, the testimony of a witness was not accepted as evidence in his own case. Though Jesus' witness was genuine, He offered the Jews twice as many witnesses as they required to verify His claims: not two witnesses but four.

Witness 1: John the Baptist. John 5:33-35

"If I testify about myself, my testimony is not true. There is another who testifies in my favour, and I know that his testimony about me is true. "You have sent to John and he has testified to the truth. Not that I accept human testimony; but I mention it that you may be saved. John was a lamp that burned and gave light, and you chose for a time to enjoy his light. 5:31-35

Jesus reminded them that they had sought confirmation from John the Baptist (1:19-27) regarding the identity of Jesus, and he had given faithful witness to Jesus. Jesus confirmed the genuineness of John's witness in that encounter (V.35).

If, like many of the ordinary people 'THE JEWS' had believed John's witness, they would now be accepting Jesus. They had failed to benefit from John's testimony.

Witness 2: Jesus' Works. John 5:36

"I have testimony weightier than that of John. For the very works that the Father has given me to finish, and which I am doing, testifies that the Father has sent me. 5:36

What works might they have witnessed up to this point?

They knew of John's testimony to Jesus (Ch. 1)

Did they know of the miracle at the wedding in Cana? (Ch. 2)

They would have known about the cleansing of the Temple. (Ch. 2)

Might they have known of Nicodemus (one of their own) having an interview with Jesus (Ch. 3) and telling Jesus of the opinion the Jews had formed about Him (*We know that you are a teacher come from God*).

They knew that Jesus was gaining and baptizing more disciples that John (Ch. 4:1). What did that tell them about Him?

They had witnessed the healing of the paralytic at the Pool of Bethesda (Ch. 5). What did that say about Jesus?

Jesus was presenting a strong and convincing case. His works were evidently the works of God.

Jesus' mark of authenticity in a disciple was very simply *'by their fruit shall ye know them'*. He challenged the Jews to apply this test to Himself. His works would show that He came from God.

Witness 3: God the Father John 5:37-38

And the Father who sent me has himself testified concerning me. You have never heard his voice nor seen his form, nor does his word dwell in you, for you do not believe the one he sent. 5:37-38

His adversaries may have known about the voice from heaven at Jesus' baptism: *'This is my beloved Son, in whom I am well-pleased.'* So he challenges their lack of integrity in ignoring the Father's testimony.

Witness 4: The Old Testament Scriptures John 5:39-47

You study the Scriptures diligently because you think that in them you possess eternal life. These are the Scriptures that testify about me, yet you refuse to come to me to have life. 5:39-40

There are none as blind as those who do not want to see. The point of Jesus' words is this:

They do not recognize the Truth himself when He stands before them.

They need to come to Him to have life, but by rejecting it they condemn themselves.

As they stood before Him he could read them like a book:

v. 40 *'you refuse to come to me'*

v. 42 *'I know that you do not have the love of God in your hearts'*

v. 43 *'I have come in my Father's name and you do not accept me'*

v. 44 *'How can you believe if your accept praise from one another*

yet make no effort to obtain the praise that comes from the only God?'

v. 45 They believed themselves to be 'Men of the Book' but Moses will be their accuser for their rejection of Jesus!

"But do not think I will accuse you before the Father.

Your accuser is Moses, on whom your hopes are set.

If you believed Moses, you would believe me, for he wrote about me.

But since you do not believe what he wrote, how are you going to believe what I say?" 5:45 -47

This is one of the key chapters, not only in John's Gospel, but also in the New Testament.

Accept it. Read it carefully. Meditate on it.

You will meet Jesus Christ in its pages.

Ask Him to reveal Himself to you.

Thank You, Heavenly Father:

For Jesus truthfulness; his enemies might reject him, yet they knew without the slightest doubt that he told them the truth;

For the multiplicity of witnesses that could be called on to bear testimony to the integrity of the words and works of Jesus;

For the weight of testimony in this section of the Scriptures that Jesus Christ is the Son of God;

For the precious Book that we know as the BIBLE; given by inspiration of God, wonderfully preserved down the centuries by the supervision of the Holy Spirit, and given to us as one of the greatest spiritual gifts we could possess, next to the gift of the Lord Jesus Christ.

In Jesus' Name, Amen

Chapter 6

John 6:1-15	**Jesus feeds the five thousand**
John 6:16-24	**Jesus walks on the water**
John 6:25-59	**Jesus the bread of life**
John 6:60-71	**Many disciples desert Jesus**

John 6: 1-15
JESUS FEEDS THE FIVE THOUSAND

This chapter with its seventy-one verses is the longest in John's Gospel. It records the first of the seven 'I AMs' of Jesus (all of which are in this gospel).

[1]Some time after this, Jesus crossed to the far shore of the Sea of Galilee (that is, the Sea of Tiberias), [2]and a great crowd of people followed him because they saw the signs he had performed by healing those who were ill. 6:1-2

Here is another instance of people following Jesus for the wrong reason. Their interest in him was no more than curiosity that craved for more miracles. Jesus did not seek this kind of following. Somehow he was able to extricate himself from the crowd and find a quiet spot where he could sit down with his disciples.

> *³Then Jesus went up on a mountainside and sat down with his disciples. ⁴The Jewish Passover Festival was near.* 6:3-4

Perhaps the size of the crowd and the fact that it had travelled with Jesus is explained by John's note: *'The Jewish Passover Festival was near.'* The majority of people were going to Jerusalem. The time spent with the disciples (and the withdrawal he had hoped for) must have been very brief because he was aware of the approaching crowds.

> *⁵When Jesus looked up and saw a great crowd coming towards him, he said to Philip, 'Where shall we buy bread for these people to eat?' ⁶He asked this only to test him, for he already had in mind what he was going to do.* 6:5-6

Here is the sign of a good leader.

Jesus was several thoughts ahead of his disciples in thinking of the needs of the crowd. It is possible that the disciples may not have had a single thought between them about providing food for the hungry. Jesus introduced the subject by asking Philip a question: *'Where shall we buy bread for these people to eat?'*

Not only was Jesus sharpening Philip's mind about the problem, John recognised it as a test question! He asked this only to test him, for he already had in mind what he was going to do.

It was Passover Time.

Crowds were converging on Jerusalem where the Passover rituals would be presided over by incompetent priests and ungodly temple leaders.

Jesus had a higher purpose in mind than the mere logistics of feeding a multitude of people.

He would provide food in the wilderness in such a way that these people would remember for as long as they lived. It would also give him the opportunity to reveal himself to them as the true bread come down from heaven.

Meanwhile, Philip's mathematical mind is turning over Jesus' question.

Whenever Philip is mentioned in the gospels he is usually analysing something, wrestling with a problem or doing mental arithmetic to work how much something will cost.

(If you want to follow this through, take a few moments and turn to John 1:43-46; John 12:20-22 and John 14:8. I think Jesus was mildly exasperated with him at times. John 14.9)

> [7]*Philip answered him, 'It would take more than half a year's wages to buy enough bread for each one to have a bite!' 6:7*

Philip failed to take Jesus' resourcefulness into his calculations, and therefore gave an unhelpful answer to the question. He might have evaded the question by blurting out: *'I think, Lord, you already know what you will do!*

A few seconds later, Andrew had an idea.

> [8]*Another of his disciples, Andrew, Simon Peter's brother, spoke up,* [9]*'Here is a boy with five small barley loaves and two small fish, but how far will they go among so many?' 6:8-9*

Alas, like his fellow-disciple, Andrew too has little faith.

Among the gospel writers John is the only one who mentions the boy. The word he used denotes 'a very small boy.' The boy had five small barley loaves (not modern pan-loaves but barley scones – translated for the benefit of my American friends – biscuits). He also had two small fish (not a trout, for example, but more likely sardines or dried fish).

In the eyes of the disciples there was nothing particularly significant in the biscuits, or the fish or the boy, except that in these circumstances they didn't amount to very much.

PHILIP pointed to the enormity of the problem (v. 7).

ANDREW pointed to the meagreness of the resources (v. 9)

JESUS accepted the boy's lunch, thanked his Heavenly Father for it and asked his blessing and used it to provide for at least 5,000 hungry people.

> *[10]Jesus said, 'Make the people sit down.' There was plenty of grass in that place, and they sat down (about five thousand men were there). [11]Jesus then took the loaves, gave thanks, and distributed to those who were seated as much as they wanted. He did the same with the fish. 6:10-11*

It was not a case of the boy's example stirring everyone present to share whatever food they had brought with them. Not at all! The commentators who first introduced this idea were demonstrating their unbelief in the miraculous aspects of Jesus' ministry.

This was a creation-miracle.

It happened when the Jesus the Creator multiplied scones and fish, and fed over 5,000 people.

> *[12]When they had all had enough to eat, he said to his disciples, 'Gather the pieces that are left over. Let nothing be wasted.' [13]So they gathered them and filled twelve baskets with the pieces of the five barley loaves left over by those who had eaten.* 6:12-13

Twelve baskets of fragments were gathered up, not only in obedience to Jesus' command, but in the tradition of the Jews *'that nothing be wasted' v. 12.* Food was not to be destroyed.

If the disciples were engaged in distributing the food – it was providential that afterwards there was still a basket for each of them. All food and drink comes from God, so here Jesus continues to do what he sees his Father doing (6:19).

What was the effect of the miracle on the people?

> *[14]After the people saw the sign Jesus performed, they began to say, 'Surely this is the Prophet who is to come into the world.' [15]Jesus, knowing that they intended to come and make him king by force, withdrew again to a mountain by himself.* 6:14-15

The people were correct in their impression. They identified Jesus as the prophet like Moses and they wanted to make him a King (Deut. 18:15).

Their grasp of who Jesus is continues to grow – but their expectation of him was wrong.

Their view was of an earthly kingship, a political entity among the nations of earth, and of course, superior to the

Romans. But they had to learn that Jesus' kingdom was not of this world.

They wanted to make him a king by force. They were not sensitive to God's timing for the revelation of his Son. Therefore Jesus withdrew to a mountain by himself.

Let us remember the details of the miraculous feeding of the Five Thousand.
It was a nature miracle performed by the incarnate Creator in order to feed a multitude of hungry people.

Thank You, Heavenly Father:

For Your glory shining through every word and action of Your Son when he was on earth;

For John's inclusion of the boy who gave his lunch to Jesus; we thank you that the service of children to Jesus will not go unblessed;

For Jesus' public acknowledgment that You are the Giver of every good and perfect gift; we too thank You for supplying our daily bread;

In Jesus' Name, Amen.

John 6: 16-24

JESUS WALKS ON THE WATER

16When evening came, his disciples went down to the lake, 17where they got into a boat and set off across the lake for Capernaum. By now it was dark, and Jesus had not yet joined them. 6:16-17

Recall where Jesus had gone at the end of the last section: v. 15

Later that evening the disciples thought of crossing the lake and going to Capernaum. Having waited for Jesus until it was dark, they cast off without him. He had not returned from his prayer vigil.

Had those seasoned fishermen not read the weather signs in the evening sky? They were about to sail into a storm, and when it hit them with screaming winds, they knew they were in danger.

18A strong wind was blowing and the waters grew rough. 19When they had rowed about three or four miles, they saw Jesus approaching the boat, walking on the water; and they were frightened. 6:18-19

The trip across the Sea of Galilee is between 6 and 7 miles, but it is reputed to be one of the most dangerous trips that one can make. And seeing Jesus coming to them walking on the water at the height of the storm didn't exactly calm them.

The solution to their crisis didn't lie with them.

[20]But he said to them, 'It is I; don't be afraid.' [21]Then they were willing to take him into the boat, and immediately the boat reached the shore where they were heading. 6:20-21

What did Jesus say that had such calming effect?

He said: 'It is I', which is the Old Testament distinctive name of Jehovah, the great 'I AM'.

Although the disciples had left without Him they were learning that he had them very much in mind and was coming to them in the storm. When they were willing to take him into the boat, the storm calmed and they arrived at the shore immediately and safely.

This was another nature-miracle,
performed by the incarnate Creator,
this time to ensure the safety of the disciples.

Here is a serious and practical question for all believers today.

Are we able to discern the presence and work of God in our lives?

Behind all blessings and sorrows, the Son of God is present and interceding for us with the Father. In all circumstances the spirit of God is present with us. We need to have eyes to see the gracious actions of God in our midst in both the joyful and painful, in both the spectacular and the ordinary.

Thank You, Heavenly Father:

For Your presence with us throughout our daily lives; not until we get to heaven shall we be able to *'bless the hand that guided and bless the heart that planned'* the course of our lives;

For our daily deliverances from dangers seen and unseen;

That *'no matter where on earth we dwell, where Jesus is, 'tis heaven there'*.

In Jesus' Name, Amen

John 6:25-59

JESUS THE BREAD OF LIFE

²²The next day the crowd that had stayed on the opposite shore of the lake realised that only one boat had been there, and that Jesus had not entered it with his disciples, but that they had gone away alone. 6:22

After the stormy night the people who were left behind on the eastern side of the lake on the previous evening wakened up to the realisation that only one boat had left for Capernaum—and Jesus had not been in the boat when it left.

How could they catch up with him again?

²³Then some boats from Tiberias landed near the place where the people had eaten the bread after the Lord had given thanks. ²⁴Once the crowd realised that neither Jesus nor his disciples were there, they got into the boats and went to Capernaum in search of Jesus. 6:23-24

Presumably those who could afford the fare boarded the boats to follow Jesus to Capernaum. Sure enough, they found him and greeted him with a question to clear up the mystery.

²⁵When they found him on the other side of the lake, they asked him, 'Rabbi, when did you get here?' 5:25

What happened next?

We need to go to v. 59 to answer this question. There the whole section from vv. 26-58 ends with the statement –

⁵⁹He said this while teaching in the synagogue in Capernaum. 6:59

That day must have been a Sabbath: because Jesus, as a visiting Rabbi had been invited to preach. His subject appears to have been God's provision of manna for the children of Israel in the desert of Sinai.

In v. 24 the people made a pretence of seeking Jesus. He forestalled their enthusiasm in v. 26.

²⁶Jesus answered, 'Very truly I tell you, you are looking for me, not because you saw the signs I performed but because you ate the loaves and had your fill. ²⁷Do not work for food that spoils, but for food that endures to eternal life, which the Son of Man will give you. For on him God the Father has placed his seal of approval.' 6:26-27

Jesus wants to redirect their fixation with food for their bodies in order to draw attention to himself as the Bread of Life.

There must have been a large number of people inside and gathered around the doors of the synagogue that day!

When we examine Jesus' teaching we discover that it was a highly interactive sermon, with the listeners talking back to him and him replying to them as he developed his message.

This was a difficult sermon to preach. Jesus worked his way through his sermon by repeatedly emphasising where necessary *'I TELL YOU THE TRUTH'* to overcome any resistance that he noticed in his hearers. See vv. 26, 32. 47 and 53.

Jesus knew that his hearers were familiar with the concept of **BREAD FROM HEAVEN** because they knew the story of the manna in Israel's history.

However, they did not understand when he spoke of himself as 'bread from heaven'. See vv. 33, 38, 41, 42. 50 and 58.

This was the truth that Jesus was preaching that day.

So how does Jesus get the people
'from where they are' to 'where he wants them to be?'

His TEXT (if we may call it that) is v. 27

[27]Do not work for food that spoils, but for food that endures to eternal life, which the Son of Man will give you. For on him God the Father has placed his seal of approval.'

<u>**Point 1 is obvious**</u>: *[27]Do not work for food that spoils,*

Even the manna given by God to the Israelites in the desert had rotted by next morning if it had not been used.

<u>**Point 2 is equally obvious**</u>: *(There is) food that endures to eternal life,*

That is to say: it does not rot but instead nourishes human life, divine life, life that continues for ever. The question is: where can it be obtained?

<u>**Point 3 follows very helpfully**</u>: *(The food that endures to eternal life) which the Son of Man will give you.'*

<u>**Point 4 is the climax:**</u>

For on him God the Father has placed his seal of approval.

The logic here is that the Son of Man can give this eternal life because the Father has authorised him to do so.

Here is what is meant by an interactive sermon.

<u>Jesus' hearers asked him:</u> 'What must we do to do the works God requires?'

<u>Jesus answered:</u> 'The work of God is this: to believe in the one he sent.'

How many congregations would respond by asking the preacher:

'What is it that God wants us to do?' v. 28

How many preachers would go to the heart of the matter and reply:

'Believe in the one he has sent?' v. 29

The congregation is trying to accept Jesus' teaching because they are asking about 'the work of God'. v. 29

But they are still missing the point: they have not picked up on Jesus' revelation of himself and of his role in giving eternal life.

The congregation has another question.

30So they asked him, 'What sign then will you give that we may see it and believe you? What will you do? 31Our ancestors ate the manna in the wilderness; as it is written: "He gave them bread from heaven to eat."'6:30-31

They are thinking of Moses' role in the story of the manna – as if it was Moses who did the giving! What role will Jesus have? Will he also give us bread from heaven to eat?

32Jesus said to them, 'Very truly I tell you, it is NOT MOSES who has given you the bread from heaven, but IT IS MY FATHER who gives you the true bread from heaven.

³³For the bread of God is the bread that comes down from heaven and gives life to the world.' 6:32-33

Jesus was an exceptional teacher.

He clarified that it was NOT MOSES who gave the Israelites bread from heaven. v. 32

He identified HIS (MY) FATHER as the giver of THE TRUE BREAD from heaven.

The manna was but a shadow of bread from heaven – THE TRUE BREAD IS A PERSON.

THE BREAD OF GOD is he who comes down from heaven and gives life to the world.

³⁴'Sir,' they said, 'always give us this bread.' John 6:34

Like Nicodemus who could only think of natural birth, and the Samaritan woman who persisted in thinking of water in the well to which she came every day to draw – these people are still fixed on an unending supply of bread for food.

Are they ready for what Jesus is about to say next?

³⁵Then Jesus declared, 'I am the bread of life. Whoever comes to me will never go hungry, and whoever believes in me will never be thirsty. 6:35

Jesus is claiming to be what one needs in order to have life and continue to live. What he said earlier about the one sent from God (v. 29) and the bread coming down from heaven (v. 33) is clearly identifies with himself.

Jesus expands the promise he made to the Samaritan woman by vowing to satisfy not only hunger but thirst as well. He makes the promise openly, not only to individuals, but to crowds of people. What is required of the crowd is that they come to him and believe in him.

³⁶But as I told you, you have seen me and still you do not believe. 6:36

What follows in vv. 37-40 is profound.

A saying of Christ about HIMSELF: v. 35

³⁵Then Jesus declared, 'I am the bread of life. Whoever comes to me will never go hungry, and whoever believes in me will never be thirsty. 6:35

A saying of Christ about THOSE WHO DO NOT BELIEVE: v. 36

³⁶But as I told you, you have seen me and still you do not believe. 6:36

A saying of Christ about THOSE WHO COME TO HIM: v. 37

³⁷All those the Father gives me will come to me, and whoever comes to me I will never drive away. 6:37

A saying of Christ about THE WILL OF HIS FATHER: vv. 37-39

³⁷All those the Father gives me will come to me, and whoever comes to me I will never drive away. ³⁸For I have come down from heaven not to do my will but to do the will of him who sent me. ³⁹And this is the will of him who sent me that I shall lose none of all those he has given me, but raise them up at the last day. 6:37-39

Salvation does not begin with a preacher's brilliance, but with God's grace drawing sinners to Jesus, making blind eyes see, enabling stubborn wills to obey the Gospel and gladly accept a wonderful Saviour. It is my role to invite everyone, without exception to come to Christ, and tell them that everyone who does come shall be received and saved.

Jesus' congregation is grumbling at this point.

[41]At this the Jews there began to grumble about him because he said, 'I am the bread that came down from heaven.' [42]They said, 'Is this not Jesus, the son of Joseph, whose father and mother we know? How can he now say, "I came down from heaven"?' 6:41-42

They could not accept the idea of his having come down from heaven (v. 41). They were in difficulty because they knew where Jesus was from (v. 42). They cannot reconcile the fact that someone having come from heaven could have earthly parents and family relatives.

The preacher replies.

[43]'Stop grumbling among yourselves,' Jesus answered. [44]'No one can come to me unless the Father who sent me draws them, and I will raise them up at the last day. [45]It is written in the Prophets: "They will all be taught by God. Everyone who has heard the Father and learned from him comes to me. 6:43-45

Jesus proceeds to substantiate the claims he has made throughout his sermon.

[46]No one has seen the Father except the one who is from God; only he has seen the Father. [47]Very truly I tell you, the one who believes has eternal life. [48]I am the bread of life. [49]Your ancestors ate the

manna in the wilderness, yet they died. ⁵⁰But here is the bread that comes down from heaven, which anyone may eat and not die. ⁵¹I am the living bread that came down from heaven. Whoever eats this bread will live for ever. This bread is my flesh, which I will give for the life of the world.' 6:46-51

Jesus spoke plainly as he delivered his sermon, piece by piece, instalment by instalment. Now that his hearers are wrestling to understand what he is teaching he doesn't soften or tone down his approach. Again, they are in difficulty.

⁵²Then the Jews began to argue sharply among themselves, 'How can this man give us his flesh to eat?' 6:52

Not only Jesus' hearers in Capernaum Synagogue, but to this day Bible readers ask the same question: 'How can this man give us his flesh to eat?'

All this was new to the people listening to Jesus. We need to note two helpful observations.

First, Jesus is not speaking literally about eating his flesh and drinking his blood. Two, Jews were forbidden to eat human flesh or drink human blood. Right away this shows that there is something different about this *'eating'* and *'drinking'*.

Two clues to Jesus' meaning lie in his words: this Bread of Life is obtained by *'coming to Him'* and by *'believing on Him.'* v. 35

Jesus is about to conclude his sermon (vv. 53-59). Notice the emphasis he places on his words: I TELL YOU THE TRUTH (also in vv. 26, 32, 47). He has brought his hearers step by step to this point. Now he is gathering up the essential strands of his teaching:

What are the issues he will lay before them?

HE GAVE THEM A RÉSUMÉ OF THE SERMON.

53Jesus said to them, 'Very truly I tell you, unless you eat the flesh of the Son of Man and drink his blood, you have no life in you. 54Whoever eats my flesh and drinks my blood has eternal life, and I will raise them up at the last day. 55For my flesh is real food and my blood is real drink. 56Whoever eats my flesh and drinks my blood remains in me, and I in them.' 6:53-56

St. Augustine expressed the meaning of Jesus' words this way: 'Believe and you have eaten.' *'Come'* to him, *and you have eaten, 'believe'* in him, *and you have eternal life.* To *eat* and *drink* of Christ is to live forever.

This believing is not mere mental assent—it is much more than that. It is an unreserved, whole-hearted acceptance of Jesus Christ the Son of God and a total dependence on him as Lord and Saviour for time and for eternity.

A believer's relationship with Jesus Christ never ends, it is eternal. Nothing in all creation can separate those he loves from him.

HE GAVE THEM A FURTHER ILLUSTRATION—THE RELATIONSHIP OF CHRIST AND HIS FATHER.

57Just as the living Father sent me and I live because of the Father, so the one who feeds on me will live because of me. 58This is the bread that came down from heaven. Your ancestors ate manna and died, but whoever feeds on this bread will live for ever.' 6:57-58

John adds a footnote: *He said this while teaching in the synagogue in Capernaum.* v. 59

Thank You, Heavenly Father:

So much about Your Son Jesus fascinates us, particularly his ability as a teacher and a leader: we are enthralled as we listen to him introducing the Jewish people to Biblical concepts that were completely new to them.

For how he dismantled their faith in Moses, as if **he** had given them bread from heaven; in order to lead them to faith in him as the new and living bread from heaven;

For Jesus' gospel invitation and the sound of his voice rising above the clamour of the crowd: *'Let anyone who is thirsty come to me and drink.'*

In Jesus' Name, Amen.

John 6:60-71

MANY DISCIPLES DESERT JESUS

What was the disciples' reaction to Jesus' sermon?

60 On hearing this, many of his disciples said, 'This is a hard teaching. Who can accept it?
61 Aware that his disciples were grumbling about this, Jesus said to them, 'Does this offend you?
62 Then what if you see the Son of Man ascend to where he was before! 6:61-62

We need to glance ahead to v. 66

66 From this time many of his disciples turned back and no longer followed him. 6:66

Here the term 'disciples' describes those who were generally found in the company of Jesus. Jesus had perfect knowledge of every heart in the crowd. He knew also that the enlightenment that individuals needed could come only from the Holy Spirit. He knew what hindered individuals from 'feeding on him'.

63 The Spirit gives life; the flesh counts for nothing.
The words I have spoken to you– they are full of the Spirit and life.
64 Yet there are some of you who do not believe.'
For Jesus had known from the beginning which of them did not believe and who would betray him.
65 He went on to say, 'This is why I told you that no one can come to me unless the Father has enabled them.'

116

From this time many of his disciples turned back and no longer followed him. 6:63-66

In days of fruitful evangelism and in days of seeming barrenness we need to remember this very comforting fact (v. 64).

Jesus invited the twelve to declare their position.

⁶⁷ 'You do not want to leave too, do you?' Jesus asked the Twelve 6:67.

Every believer understands exactly what the Lord required of Peter. This one of those golden moments when a believer must shine brightly. What will Peter's answer be?

⁶⁸Simon Peter answered him, 'Lord, to whom shall we go? You have the words of eternal life. ⁶⁹We have come to believe and to know that you are the Holy One of God.' 6:68-69

Did anyone in the crowd overhear what Peter said? Peter's answer is a good example of a disciple who has discovered and eaten of 'the Bread that came down from heaven.'

Our Lord's final word on this occasion is an instance of mixed feelings, and gives us a glimpse into the issues that pressed upon Jesus' soul and spirit.

⁷⁰Then Jesus replied, 'Have I not chosen you, the Twelve? Yet one of you is a devil!' ⁷¹(He meant Judas, the son of Simon Iscariot, who, though one of the Twelve, was later to betray him.) 6:70-71

Thank You, Heavenly Father:

For the two creation-miracles recorded in John 5: the feeding
of the five thousand, and the stilling of the storm on the Sea
of Galilee;

For the clear explanation of Jesus' authority, based on the filial
relationship between God the Father and Jesus his Son;

For the authority that God has given his Son: he does what he
sees his Father doing, he gives life to whom he is pleased
to give it, he had entrusted all judgment to the Son, and resurrection is a prerogative of the Son;

In Jesus' Name, Amen.

Chapter 7

John 7:1-13

JESUS GOES TO THE FEAST OF TABERNACLES

Chapters 7 to 10 are the long central section of the gospel covering the final year of Jesus' ministry, from the second Passover at which he fed the crowd until the third Passover during which he was crucified.

'Discretion is the better part of valour' it is said. This governed Jesus' movements and so he remained in Galilee rather than itinerating throughout Judea.

After this, Jesus went around in Galilee. He did not want to go about in Judea because the Jewish leaders there were looking for a way to kill him. 7:1

He knew the Jews there were waiting to take his life, but above that consideration it was not the Father's appointed time for him to move about openly, so he purposely stayed away from Judea

But when the Jewish Feast of Tabernacles was near, Jesus' brothers said to him, "Leave Galilee and go to Judea, so that your disciples may see the works you do.
No-one who wants to become a public figure acts in secret.
Since you are doing these things, show yourself to the world." For even his own brothers did not believe in him. 7:2-5

What was the Feast of Tabernacles?

It was also called the Feast of Booths commemorating God's care of the Israelites during their forty years of wandering in the desert. It was held in early October and doubled up as a Harvest Festival. The pilgrims lived in booths made of branches or small tents –hence the name 'The Feast of Tabernacles'. It was one of three feasts every mature Jewish male was expected to attend. It ran for seven days and was reputedly the most popular of the festivals.

It had special features such as the water-drawing and the lamp-lighting rites, which were performed each day in the temple. Jesus referred to these in his teaching.

During the Festival the people gave thanks for the rainfall which nourished the harvest, but also looked forward to the day when God's Spirit would be poured out at the coming of the kingdom of God.

Jesus' brothers were unable to understand why he didn't go up to Jerusalem where he could have unlimited publicity and perform many miracles.

Jesus' brothers (he had siblings) were not governed in their movements as he was. While Jesus was virgin born, the New Testament nowhere speaks of the perpetual virginity of Mary his mother or suggests that Jesus was an only child.

Whatever the motives of his brothers, Jesus had his reasons for staying in and around Galilee.

Therefore Jesus told them, "The right time for me has not yet come; for you any time is right. The world cannot hate you, but it hates me because I testify that what it does is evil. You go to the Feast. I am not yet going up to this Feast, because for me the right time has not yet come." Having said this, he stayed in Galilee. 7:6-9

'Show yourself to the world' they had urged him, thinking like the worldly men they were. *'For me the right time has not yet come,'* he answered.

It may have been a matter of days later that Jesus went up to the feast secretly. Not only had he been correct to exercise caution, there was also malicious gossip among the crowds in Jerusalem.

However, after his brothers had left for the Feast, he went also, not publicly, but in secret. Now at the Feast the Jews were watching for him and asking, "Where is that man?" Among the crowds there was widespread whispering about him. Some said, "He is a good man." Others replied, "No, he deceives the people." But no-one would say anything publicly about him for fear of the Jews. 7:10-13

Had deception been proven, it would have been a capital offence (Deut. 13:1-6).

John 7: 14-24

JESUS TEACHES AT THE FESTIVAL

Not until halfway through the Feast did Jesus go up to the temple courts and begin to teach.
The Jews were amazed and asked, "How did this man get such learning without having studied?" 7:14-15

He had never been enrolled at one of the rabbinic centres of learning. Jesus answered the question openly and confidently.

Jesus answered, "My teaching is not my own. It comes from him who sent me. If anyone chooses to do God's will, he will find out whether my teaching comes from God or whether I speak on my own. 7:16-17

He then added a further imprimatur:

He who speaks on his own does so to gain honour for himself, but he who works for the honour of the one who sent him is a man of truth; there is nothing false about him. 7:18

There is no way to test a claim to divine revelation other than this one. He is inviting the crowd to put his teaching to the test.

Then he turns the matter of submitting to divine authority against the Jews:

Has not Moses given you the law?
Yet not one of you keeps the law.

Why are you trying to kill me?" 7:19

They are breaking Moses' Law themselves by their plots to kill him.

"You are demon-possessed," the crowd answered. "Who is trying to kill you?" 7:20

The crowd seems to be unaware of the plots their leaders have hatched against him. Here John distinguishes the masses from their leaders.

Jesus said to them, "I did one miracle, and you are all astonished. 7:21-24

He was referring to the healing of the paralytic at the pool of Bethesda on the Sabbath day.

Yet, because Moses gave you circumcision (though actually it did not come from Moses, but from the patriarchs), you circumcise a child on the Sabbath.

The rite of circumcision involved removing the foreskins from male children which on the flick of a knife made them less than *'whole'*.

Now if a child can be circumcised on the Sabbath so that the law of Moses may not be broken, why are you angry with me for healing the whole man on the Sabbath?

Jesus had made a paralytic whole again, after thirty-eight years, so that he could take up his mat and walk. For this the Jews wanted to kill him.

Stop judging by mere appearances, and make a right judgment. "7:24

Their judgment of Jesus was not *'right'* judgment i.e. it was skewed because it was affected by their sinful prejudices and therefore could not possibly be right judgment. Cf: Deut 16:18-20.

John 7: 25-44

IS JESUS THE CHRIST?

At that point some of the people of Jerusalem began to ask, "Isn't this the man they are trying to kill?
Here he is, speaking publicly, and they are not saying a word to him. Have the authorities really concluded that he is the Christ?
But we know where this man is from; 7:25-27

In the minds of some of the people Jesus preaching publicly and without hindrance caused them to believe that the authorities had concluded that he was the Christ!

Yet others, knowing something of Jesus' birth and upbringing couldn't think of him as the Messiah (v. 27). Their problem was that they knew him *'after the flesh'* to use Paul's term in 2 Cor. 5:16-17.

Wherefore henceforth know we no man after the flesh: yea, though we have known Christ after the flesh, yet now henceforth know we him no more. Therefore if any man be in Christ, he is a new creature: old things are passed away; behold, all things are become new. 2 Cor. 5:16-17 (KJV)
So from now on we regard no-one from a worldly point of view. Though we once regarded Christ in this way, we do so no longer. Therefore, if anyone is in Christ, he is a new creation; the old has gone, the new has come! 2 Cor. 5:16-17 (NIV-UK)

Then Jesus, still teaching in the temple courts, cried out,

"Yes, you know me, and you know where I am from. I am not here on my own, but he who sent me is true. You do not know him, but I know him because I am from him and he sent me." 7:28-29

This claim incensed the authorities, who attempt to seize him, but they were divinely frustrated.

At this they tried to seize him, but no-one laid a hand on him, because his time had not yet come. 7:30

Perhaps the authorities were intimidated by the popular support for Jesus in the crowd, unaware that they were being restrained from heaven. 7:31

Still, many in the crowd put their faith in him. They said,

"When the Christ comes, will he perform more signs than this man?"

The faith of many in the crowd cannot be regarded as saving faith. It was more like admiration for Jesus. Knowing that this opinion was circulating drove the authorities to arrest Jesus.

The Pharisees heard the crowd whispering such things about him. Then the chief priests and the Pharisees sent temple guards to arrest him. 7:32

While the guards are gone 'the Jews' (i.e. official Judaism) talk about Jesus.

Jesus said, "I am with you for only a short time, and then I go to the one who sent me. You will look for me, but you will not find me; and where I am, you cannot come."
The Jews said to one another, "Where does this man intend to go that we cannot find him? Will he go where our people live scattered among the Greeks, and teach the Greeks?

What did he mean when he said, 'You will look for me, but you will not find me,' and 'where I am, you cannot come'?" 7:33-36

It is clear that Jesus has the Jews guessing. They do not understand him.

Meanwhile, Jesus is still preaching.

On the last and greatest day of the Feast, Jesus stood and said in a loud voice,

"If anyone is thirsty, let him come to me and drink. Whoever believes in me, as the Scripture has said, streams of living water will flow from within him." 7:37-39

Here John inserts a helpful paragraph.

By this he meant the Spirit, whom those who believed in him were later to receive. Up to that time the Spirit had not been given, since Jesus had not yet been glorified. 7:39

At this point we need to find the reason why Jesus mentioned thirst, and drinking, and streams of living water.

Every day during the Feast of Tabernacles an appointed person had carried water in a gold pitcher from the Pool of Siloam to be poured into a basin at the foot of the altar.

It symbolised prayer for rain.

The rabbis associated the custom with Isaiah 12:3

'With joy you shall draw water from the wells of salvation.'

On the seventh day the water pouring was accompanied by the blowing of gold trumpets, singing sacred songs and the ordinary people waving their palm leaves, myrtle and willow branches, and chanting the Hallel Psalms (113-118)

v. 37 notes that it was the last great day of the Feast.

We can imagine Jesus, standing somewhere adjacent to the Temple Courts in full view of the various ceremonies, watching the pouring of the water at the foot of the altar, lifting up his voice and declaring words that had never been heard in such an authoritative way before:

> *"If anyone is thirsty, let him come to me and drink.*
> *Whoever believes in me, as the Scripture has said,*
> *streams of living water will flow from within him."*

vv. 40-44 record various views about Jesus being expressed in the crowd.

> *On hearing his words, some of the people said, "Surely this man is the Prophet." Others said, "He is the Christ." Still others asked, "How can the Christ come from Galilee?*
> *Does not the Scripture say that the Christ will come from David's family and from Bethlehem, the town where David lived?"*
>
> *Thus the people were divided because of Jesus. Some wanted to seize him, but no-one laid a hand on him. 7:40-44*

John 7: 45-52

UNBELIEF OF THE JEWISH LEADERS

The Temple Police return to their masters.

'Official Judaism' didn't know how to proceed. They were powerless – and Jesus was still at large.

Finally the temple guards went back to the chief priests and Pharisees, who asked them, "Why didn't you bring him in?"
"No-one ever spoke the way this man does," the guards declared.
"You mean he has deceived you also?" the Pharisees retorted.
"Has any of the rulers or of the Pharisees believed in him?
No! But this mob that knows nothing of the law – there is a curse on them." 7:45-49

However, whether Jesus or the mob – the officials dismissed both as fools who knew nothing about the law!

In the confusion a voice was heard making a plea for sanity and for legality. It was Nicodemus who had intervened!

We know two things about him: (1) he had gone to Jesus earlier (Ch. 3) and (2) he was a member of the Sanhedrin (v. 50).

Nicodemus, who had gone to Jesus earlier and who was one of their own number, asked, "Does our law condemn a man without first hearing him to find out what he is doing?"
They replied, "Are you from Galilee, too? Look into it, and you will find that a prophet does not come out of Galilee." 7:50-52

Nicodemus courageously challenged his colleagues' dismissal of Jesus, quoting the widely acknowledged principle of Jewish law viz. the right of the accused to have due representation (v. 51).

His colleagues summarily dismissed him with a jibe about Jesus' Galilean origin. (v. 52). The Pharisees didn't have respect for Galileans.

Nicodemus was not mistaken, because the Jews held that six prophets- Jonah, Hosea, Nahum, Elijah, Elisha and Amos – had come from Galilee.

Thank You, Heavenly Father:

For the wisdom and initiative of Jesus in making use of the Jewish Festivals and their associated rituals in revealing himself to the people of Israel (e.g. bread, water, light and so on);

For the ways in which the devious methods of the Jewish leaders to arrest and kill Jesus all met with failure;

For the way in which the Holy Spirit has transformed our view of things, not least in the way we regard people; not from a worldly point of view, but as souls that are precious to You because of what Jesus achieved at Calvary for our salvation and theirs;

In Jesus' Name, Amen.

Chapter 8

OMIT JOHN 7:53 TO 8:11

In some editions of the KJV a marginal note, and in the NIV an explanatory note, has been inserted to explain the absence of John 7:53 to 8:11 from the published text. The reason arises from MSS evidence. The earliest manuscripts and many other ancient witnesses do not have John 7:33-8:11.

Equally convincing, none of the early church fathers who wrote commentaries on John's gospel include it. There can be no real doubt that it was not an original part of John. In any case, the section beginning with John 8:12 follows seamlessly from 7:52.

John 8: 12-20

DISPUTE OVER JESUS' TESTIMONY

Jesus is still in Jerusalem at the Feast of Tabernacles. Why is he now adding *'light of the world'* to his titles?

> *When Jesus spoke again to the people, he said, "I am the light of the world. Whoever follows me will never walk in darkness, but will have the light of life." 8:12*

The feast had two symbols: water and light. Water reminded the Jews of how God miraculously provided water from the rock in the desert. Light reminded them of the pillar of cloud and fire by which God led the people on their journey. Jesus had used the water ceremonies to draw attention himself (7:37) when he said *'If anyone is thirsty, let him come to me and drink. Whoever believes in me, as the Scripture has said, streams of living water will flow from within him.'*

> *When Jesus spoke again to the people, he said, "I am the light of the world. Whoever follows me will never walk in darkness, but will have the light of life." 8:12*

At the end of the first day in the 'court of women' four golden lamps were lit amid great rejoicing. Singing and celebration with music continued through the nights of the feast, with the light in the temple illuminating the entire city.

There was not a courtyard in Jerusalem that was not lit up by the light of the festivities. Pious men and men of good deeds would dance around with burning torches in their hands, singing songs and praises, while the Levites played harps, lyres, cymbals, trumpets and innumerable musical instruments.

The official reaction to Jesus' tremendous claim is predictable. The Pharisees pounce:

> *The Pharisees challenged him, "Here you are, appearing as your own witness; your testimony is not valid." 8:13*

Previously Jesus had admitted (5:31) *'if I testify about myself, my testimony is not valid'*. He immediately provided no less than four witnesses who could confirm that his claims were legitimate.

Now, on this occasion he quickly refers to his witness: his Father in heaven.

> *Jesus answered, "Even if I testify on my own behalf, my testimony is valid, for I know where I came from and where I am going. But you have no idea where I come from or where I am going.*
> *You judge by human standards; I pass judgment on no-one. But if I do judge, my decisions are right, because I am not alone. I stand with the Father, who sent me.*
> *In your own Law it is written that the testimony of two witnesses is true. I am one who testifies for myself; my other witness is the Father, who sent me." 8:14-18*

The Jews reply with an obvious question.

> *Then they asked him, "Where is your father?"*

"You do not know me or my Father," Jesus replied.
"If you knew me, you would know my Father also." 8:19

As men who were the official guardians and teachers of Israel they were strangers to the living God. However Jesus is indicating that the way to know God is now open to them. Their human judgments reflect the reality that they are merely worldly men holding religious office in Judaism.

He spoke these words while teaching in the temple area near the place where the offerings were put. Yet no-one seized him, because his time had not yet come. 8:20

Jesus stands alone because of who he is. He doesn't make it easy for their prejudiced minds to understand him. There will be no dilution of his claims for anyone.

John 8:21-30

DISPUTE OVER WHO JESUS IS

Once more Jesus said to them, "I am going away, and you will look
for me, and you will die in your sin. Where I go, you cannot come."
This made the Jews ask, "Will he kill himself? Is that why he says,
'Where I go, you cannot come'?" 8:21-22

He is making them aware of their sin.

He continues to draw them out

He appeals to his divine origin.

But he continued, "You are from below; I am from above.
You are of this world; I am not of this world.
I told you that you would die in your sins; if you do not believe that
I am the one I claim to be, you will indeed die in your sins." 8:23-24

He has said clearly that he comes from the heavenly world.

In exasperation with him they ask the essential question.

"Who are you?" they asked.
"Just what I have been claiming all along," Jesus replied.
"I have much to say in judgment of you. But he who sent me is reli-
able, and what I have heard from him I tell the world." They did
not understand that he was telling them about his Father. So Jesus
said, "When you have lifted up the Son of Man, then you will know
that I am the one I claim to be and that I do nothing on my own but
speak just what the Father has taught me. The one who sent me
is with me; he has not left me alone, for I always do what pleases
him." Even as he spoke, many put their faith in him. 8:25-30

J esus authority was unassailable. In total submission to his
father's will he was able to testify with authority. He was
speaking what his father gave him to speak.

While this confrontation was going on between Jesus and
the Pharisees, there were *'many (who) put their faith in him'*.
(v. 30)

Who were these people?

John 8: 31-41

CHILDREN OF ABRAHAM OR CHILDREN OF THE DEVIL?

We have never been slaves of anyone. How can you say that we shall be set free?" 8:33

Jesus clarifies their bondage.

Jesus replied, "I tell you the truth, everyone who sins is a slave to sin. Now a slave has no permanent place in the family, but a son belongs to it forever. So if the Son sets you free, you will be free indeed." 8:34-36

Jesus reply acknowledges that they are children of Abraham—*nevertheless they are slaves to sin*. You are Abraham's children *but you are ready to kill me, because you have no room for my word.*

Why are the Pharisees and Jesus poles apart?

"I am telling you what I have seen in the Father's presence, and you do what you have heard from your father." 8:38

Watch their reaction:

"Abraham is our father," they answered.
"If you were Abraham's children," said Jesus, "then you would do the things Abraham did.

"As it is, you are determined to kill me, a man who has told you the truth that I heard from God." 8:39-41

In that moment I think they caught his point:-

"We are not illegitimate children," they protested. "The only Father we have is God himself." 8:41
"In fact, they were doing the works of their father, the devil."

The Jews are adamant about their religious credentials. Then Jesus deflates their religious pride:

Abraham did not do such things. "You are doing the things your own father does." 8:44

John 8: 42-47

JESUS CONDEMNS THEM AS CHILDREN OF THE DEVIL

Jesus said to them, "If God were your Father, you would love me, for I came from God and now am here. I have not come on my own; but he sent me. 8:42

Their ears and understanding are closed up–the devil has made them deaf to the words of God.

"Why is my language not clear to you? Because you are unable to hear what I say. You belong to your father, the devil, and you want to carry out your father's desire. He was a murderer from the beginning, not holding to the truth, for there is no truth in him. When he lies, he speaks his native language, for he is a liar and the father of lies. Yet because I tell the truth, you do not believe me!" 8:43-45

When God gives someone a character reference we may be sure that it is true! These men were children of Abraham by natural descent; nevertheless they were children of the devil and gave evidence of it by their hatred of the truth and their determination to kill Jesus the Son of God.

"Yet because I tell the truth, you do not believe me! Can any of you prove me guilty of sin? If I am telling the truth, why don't you believe me? He who belongs to God hears what God says. The reason you do not hear is that you do not belong to God." 8:45-47 The Jews answered him, "Aren't we right in saying that you are a Samaritan and demon-possessed?"

"I am not possessed by a demon," said Jesus, "but I honour my Father and you dishonour me" 8:48-49

They dared to call him a Samaritan—a very deep insult. In their view Samaritans did not have the same pure religious inheritance that the Jews had.

John 8:48–59

JESUS' CLAIMS ABOUT HIMSELF.

They further accused him of demon-possession. This had happened before (7:20; 8:52; 10:20) and would be repeated. Jesus passion was the complete opposite to demon-possession: his passion was to serve the living God and to further his honour. (v. 49).

> *I am not seeking glory for myself; but there is one who seeks it, and he is the judge. I tell you the truth, if anyone keeps my word, he will never see death."* 8:50-51

Jesus' glory is a matter for the Father, who seeks the Son's glory in the present and will realize it in the future at the judgment when those who have kept Jesus' word will pass into eternal life.

> *At this the Jews exclaimed, "Now we know that you are demon-possessed!*
> *Abraham died and so did the prophets, yet you say that if anyone keeps your word, he will never taste death.*
> *Are you greater than our father Abraham? He died, and so did the prophets. Who do you think you are?"* 8:52-53

Before answering that question directly, Jesus affirms his claim to know the Father. The Father is the key to who Jesus is. He is the one the Father has sent into the world, in fulfilment of the ancient promises to Israel.

> *Jesus replied, "If I glorify myself, my glory means nothing.*

My Father, whom you claim as your God, is the one who glori-
fies me.
Though you do not know him, I know him.
If I said I did not, I would be a liar like you,
but I do know him and keep his word." 8:54-55

Now follows the punch-line and they don't see it coming!

"Your father Abraham rejoiced at the thought of seeing my day; he
saw it and was glad."
"You are not yet fifty years old," the Jews said to him,
"and you have seen Abraham!" 8:56-57

Abraham received the promises of God by faith, and in that
sense *'rejoiced at the thought of seeing my day.'*

"I tell you the truth," Jesus answered, "before Abraham was born,
I AM!" At this, they picked up stones to stone him, but Jesus hid
himself, slipping away from the temple grounds. 8:58-59

They heard Jesus use the great name of God 'I AM', revealed
to Moses at the Burning Bush centuries before. They now know
beyond a doubt that Jesus claims to be GOD'.

This is one of Jesus' clearest self-pronouncements of his Deity.

Thank You, Heavenly Father:

For the Holy Scriptures, so divinely inspired and wonderfully
preserved. We appreciate these occasional notes from the
translators whose painstaking work ensures that we have a
reliable Bible;

For the 'more than adequate' witnesses to the integrity of Jesus'
person, his words and works;

For the fact that You are the key to understanding who Jesus is.

For the witness of Abraham to Jesus the Son of God!

In Jesus' Name, Amen,

Chapter 9

THE SIXTH SIGN

John 9:1-12	Jesus heals a man born blind
John 9:13-34	The Pharisees investigate the healing
John 9:35-41	Spiritual blindness

As he went along, he saw a man blind from birth. His disciples asked him, "Rabbi, who sinned, this man or his parents, that he was born blind?" J 9:1-2

Life has always had its mysteries, particularly in the area of the health of children. It is such a miracle when we hold a new-born child in our arms knowing that it is perfectly whole in mind and body. We thank God for it.

Childbirth is an area in which so many complications can arise. When a gynaecologist tells the parents of a new-born baby that there is some complication, inevitably they ask *'Why?'*

It is natural to expect that the parents of the man to whom Jesus restored sight asked the question: *'Why?'*

There are attitudes and opinions that we ought to avoid because they are wrong and unhelpful. Something of the folk-lore of the time is reflected in the question that the disciples put to Jesus, *"Rabbi, who sinned, this man or his parents, that he was born blind?"* This was the Pharisees' theology of suffering.

Jesus reply was *'a faith-answer'* to their question.

"Neither this man nor his parents sinned," said Jesus, "but this happened so that the work of God might be displayed in his life." 9:3

Jesus had complete confidence that his Father knew the reason for the man's blindness. It wasn't an answer that would satisfy an unbelieving mind, indeed some believing minds might struggle to accept it.

Nevertheless it is an answer that provides *'a holding position'* until such time as God may be pleased to reveal the reason why.

Sin has produced a suffering world, but an individual's personal suffering is not always attributable to his or her personal sin. Sometimes it may be due to drunken driving or sexual promiscuity, for instance. But the Scriptures prohibit us from accepting these as universal reasons. This was the issue between Job and his friends, and much of the lesson of the book of Job is God's dismissal of a simplistic theology of suffering. It is here dismissed by Jesus.

As long as it is day, we must do the work of him who sent me. Night is coming, when no-one can work. While I am in the world, I am the light of the world." 9:3-5

There is an urgency in Jesus' words. He knew that his Father's work included the healing of this blind man. The emphasis on his claim to be *'the light of the world'* says as much. The man's blindness in close proximity to him who is *'the light of the world'* suggests the probability of a healing miracle.

Having said this, he spat on the ground, made some mud with the saliva, and put it on the man's eyes. "Go," he told him, "wash in the Pool of Siloam" (this word means Sent). So the man went and washed, and came home seeing. 9:6-7

The Lord didn't have to use means; he could have healed the man with a word or a touch. The use of saliva for medicinal purposes was common in the ancient world and Jesus himself used it in his healings at times (Mark 7:33 – in the healing of a deaf and mute man; Mark 8:23 – in the healing of a blind man at Bethsaida).

The man had no hesitation in obeying Jesus' instruction. So he went – and washed – and came home seeing.

As always – the neighbours talked about what had happened.

His neighbours and those who had formerly seen him begging asked, "Isn't this the same man who used to sit and beg?" Some claimed that he was. Others said, "No, he only looks like him." But he himself insisted, "I am the man." 9:8-9

In the 1859 Revival in Ulster a hymn was written – and sung with gusto – *'Whene'er we meet you always say 'What's the news? What's the news?'* It reflected the enthusiasm with which people asked about the latest happenings in the revival. How would our society react to another revival? It would be refreshing to hear the general public talking and enquiring about what God the Holy Spirit was doing!

"How then were your eyes opened?" they demanded.
He replied, "The man they call Jesus made some mud and put it on my eyes. He told me to go to Siloam and wash. So I went and washed, and then I could see." "Where is this man?" they asked him. "I don't know," he said. 9:10-12

The man couldn't identify his healer for the simple reason that he had *'never set eyes on him'*.

John 9: 13-34

THE PHARISEES INVESTIGATE
THE HEALING

They brought to the Pharisees the man who had been blind. Now the day on which Jesus had made the mud and opened the man's eyes was a Sabbath. Therefore the Pharisees also asked him how he had received his sight. "He put mud on my eyes," the man replied, "and I washed, and now I see." 9:13-15

It would be wrong for us to attach any malicious intent in the neighbours going to the Pharisees to ask for an explanation for the miracle. The people looked to them as their religious leaders. It would appear that until the man was brought before them the Pharisees were in ignorance of his healing (v. 14). Naturally, they questioned him.

Some of the Pharisees said, "This man is not from God, for he does not keep the Sabbath." But others asked, "How can a sinner do such miraculous signs?" So they were divided. 9:16

Their opinions and condemnatory spirit were predictable.

Finally they turned again to the blind man, "What have you to say about him? It was your eyes he opened."
The man replied, "He is a prophet." 9:17
They still did not believe that he had been blind and had received his sight until they sent for the man's parents. "Is this your son?"

146

they asked. "Is this the one you say was born blind? How is it that
now he can see?" 9:18-19

Now it is the Jews who are blind. They refused to accept a
miraculous healing with the evidence of a seeing man standing
before them.

"We know he is our son," the parents answered, "and we know he
was born blind.
But how he can see now, or who opened his eyes, we don't know.
Ask him. He is of age; he will speak for himself."
His parents said this because they were afraid of the Jewish leaders
who already had decided that anyone who acknowledged that
Jesus was the Christ would be put out of the synagogue.
That was why his parents said, "He is of age; ask him." 9:20-23

Evidently the Pharisees ruled by fear.

A second time they summoned the man who had been blind. "Give
glory to God," they said. "We know this man is a sinner."
He replied, "Whether he is a sinner or not, I don't know. One thing
I do know. I was blind but now I see!" 9:24-25

The man had little theology; but he had a lot of honesty!

Then they asked him, "What did he do to you? How did he open
your eyes?" He answered, "I have told you already and you did not
listen. Why do you want to hear it again? Do you want to become
his disciples, too?" 9:26-27

These Pharisees were false shepherds. They hadn't a grain
of compassion between them. They knew nothing about compassion and a lot about interrogation!

Then they hurled insults at him and said, ²⁸"You are this fellow's
disciple! We are disciples of Moses!

147

[32]Nobody has ever heard of opening the eyes of a man born blind. [33]If this man were not from God, he could do nothing." 9:31-33

The Pharisees treated the man with scorn and contempt.

[34]To this they replied, "You were steeped in sin at birth; how dare you lecture us!" And they threw him out. 9:34

That is to say—they threw him out of the temple. He was excommunicated.

John 9: 35-41

SPIRITUAL BLINDNESS

In complete contrast to the Jewish leaders – who thought nothing of throwing a man out of the temple, here is Jesus, the true shepherd of Israel 'pastoring' him.

> *Jesus heard that they had thrown him out, and when he found him, he said, "Do you believe in the Son of Man?"*
> *"Who is he, sir?" the man asked. "Tell me so that I may believe in him."*
> *Jesus said, "You have now seen him; in fact, he is the one speaking with you." Then the man said, "Lord, I believe," and he worshipped him* 9:35-38

The word means that he prostrated himself before Jesus.

Here, in this former blind man, we have the anticipation of Thomas' dramatic confession of Jesus as Lord.

Meanwhile, what about the Pharisees? Has Jesus anything to say to them?

> *Jesus said, "For judgment I have come into this world, so that the blind will see and those who see will become blind."*
> *Some Pharisees who were with him heard him say this and asked, "What? Are we blind too?"*
> *Jesus said, "If you were blind, you would not be guilty of sin; but now that you claim you can see, your guilt remains.* 9:39-41

The sun that melts wax, hardens clay. Jesus' opponents had hard hearts. Such hardness of heart darkened their minds and alienated them from the life of God. They are ones who think they know God, but do not recognise Jesus for who he is. Spiritual blindness is their real sin. In their judgment and condemnation of Jesus they stand self-judged and self-condemned.

Thank You, Heavenly Father:

For Jesus' ministry while on earth among people like us; our needs involved a significant amount of healing. This is something for which we are very grateful. We thank you for the availability of medication, but healing comes to us from Your Son Jesus;

That this man, already burdened by blindness, wasn't required to upgrade in any way before Jesus ministered to him. For instance he didn't know his healer's name. That was not a disadvantage – because Jesus accepted him without requiring specialist knowledge of any kind;

The Lord Jesus had this man in his mind, and was aware of the behaviour of the Jews. So he made a point of finding him when the Jews no longer gave him 'house-room'. *What a friend we have in Jesus!'*

In Jesus' Name, Amen.

Chapter 10

John 10:1-21

THE GOOD SHEPHERD AND HIS SHEEP

Jesus now puts the events of chapter 9 into perspective by contrasting himself, the Good Shepherd, with the Pharisees, whom he identifies with the evil shepherds of Ezekiel 34. The Pharisees have expelled from God's flock the man whom Christ himself enlightened. They are scattering the sheep whom Christ came to gather.

In this way, Jesus' estrangement from official Judaism is further developed as he calls into being a people who follow him rather than the leaders of Israel.

> *"Verily I tell you Pharisees, anyone who does not enter the sheep-*
> *fold by the gate, but climbs in by some other way, is a thief and a*
> *robber.*
> *The one who enters by the gate is the shepherd of his sheep.*
> *The gatekeeper opens the gate for him, and the sheep listen to his*
> *voice. He calls his own sheep by name and leads them out.*

When he has brought out all his own, he goes on ahead of them,
and his sheep follow him because they know his voice.
But they will never follow a stranger; in fact, they will run away
from him because they do not recognise a stranger's voice."
Jesus used this figure of speech, but the Pharisees did not under-
stand what he was telling them. 10:1-6

Jesus is drawing a word-picture of the Good Shepherd in the hearing of the Pharisees i.e. official Judaism. He is contrasting himself with the false shepherds with whom he has just tangled, and whose dereliction has been apparent in the case of the newly healed blind-man. By contrast with the Good Shepherd the *'thieves and robbers'* stand self-condemned.

Therefore Jesus said again, "Very truly I tell you, I am the gate for
the sheep. All who have come before me were thieves and robbers,
but the sheep have not listened to them. I am the gate; whoever
enters through me will be saved. He will come in and go out, and
find pasture. The thief comes only to steal and kill and destroy; I
have come that they may have life, and have it to the full. 10:7-10

Here Jesus says that he is both the gate to the enclosure and the shepherd of the sheep. This is the familiar figure of the shepherd sitting in the entrance to the fold—and becomes himself—'the gate.'

These verses say that his sheep are secured and nourished under his care.

V. 10 states another feature of Christ's sheep:

'I am come that they might have life, and have it to the full.'

Life to the full is the eternal life of the kingdom. It is glimpsed briefly in Eden, and seen in the vision in Revelation as a city coming down from God, the holy dwelling of God with his people. It is the life for which we were created.

"I am the good shepherd. The good shepherd lays down his life for the sheep. The hired hand is not the shepherd and does not own the sheep. So when he sees the wolf coming, he abandons the sheep and runs away. Then the wolf attacks the flock and scatters it. The man runs away because he is a hired hand and cares nothing for the sheep. "I am the good shepherd; I know my sheep and my sheep know me— just as the Father knows me and I know the Father— and I lay down my life for the sheep. 10:11-15

vv. 11-15 speak of how these blessings are won. Shepherding can be a dangerous occupation. The shepherd has to place himself between the sheep and those who would harm them. He hazards his life to protect the flock. Jesus is speaking of Calvary where he will in fact lay down his life for the sheep.

Jesus identifies his flock.

I have other sheep that are not of this sheepfold. I must bring them also. They too will listen to my voice, and there shall be one flock and one shepherd. 10:16

In the Old Testament God's flock was Israel. This being so, who are the *'other sheep'*? This can only be a reference to the Gentile nations among whom the Shepherd will find many sheep and add them to his flock. So Jesus' vision encompasses the whole world. John saw the flock of Christ in his vision on the isle of Patmos in Rev. 7:9-10.

After this I looked and there before me was a great multitude that no-one could count, from every nation, tribe, people and language, standing before the throne and in front of the Lamb. They were wearing white robes and were holding palm branches in their hands. And they cried out in a loud voice: "Salvation belongs to our God, who sits on the throne, and to the Lamb." Revelation 7:9-10

Jesus takes us behind the scenes – and we learn what the world cannot know – the ongoing relationship between the Father and the Son in relation to the world's salvation.

The reason my Father loves me is that I lay down my life—only to take it up again. No-one takes it from me, but I lay it down of my own accord. I have authority to lay it down and authority to take it up again. This command I received from my Father." 10:17-18

1. The self-sacrifice of the Son is related to the Father's love for the Son. The love of the Father for the Son and the Son for the Father finds a fulfilment in the heart of God as the Son gives himself for us.

2. Jesus' self-sacrifice for us was a voluntary one. 'No-one takes my life from me, but I lay it down. Thus the control, as far as Jesus' sacrifice and death are concerned, lies not with Judas, or Caiaphas, or Pilate, or the Sanhedrim, but with Jesus himself. He gave himself freely.

3. Jesus' vision embraces not just his death but also the resurrection that will follow (18)

Indeed, the death of such a One as Christ, the well-beloved Son of God, demands the resurrection as its necessary sequel. In a very profound but practical sense *'it was not possible for death to keep its hold on him.* (Acts 2:24)

Death could not keep its prey: Jesus my Saviour; He tore the bars away: Jesus my Lord.

4. Jesus' road to the cross, his voluntary self-sacrifice and his resurrection—all of this Jesus will do in obedience to His Father. This command I received from my Father. v. 18.

Meantime, what is the effect on the Jews?

The Jews who heard these words were again divided.
Many of them said, "He is demon-possessed and raving mad. Why listen to him?"
But others said, "These are not the sayings of a man possessed by a demon. Can a demon open the eyes of the blind?" 10:19-21

There was division, as we might expect. There was continued blasphemy as the Jews attributed demon-possession to him. They are becoming increasingly frustrated. They have a deepening resolve to close their eyes to the light.

The issue becomes personal when we ask ourselves the question:

'What do we think of Jesus?'

John 10: 22-42

THE UNBELIEF OF THE JEWS

Then came the Festival of Dedication at Jerusalem. It was winter, and Jesus was in the temple area walking in Solomon's Colonnade. 10:22-23

In winter weather Solomon's Colonnade provided some shelter and Jesus would go there to teach and preach.

The Jews gathered round him, saying, "How long will you keep us in suspense? If you are the Christ, tell us plainly." 10:24

There could be only one answer to their question.

Jesus answered, "I did tell you, but you do not believe. The miracles I do in my Father's name testify about me, but you do not believe because you are not my sheep. 10:25-26

Their antipathy to Jesus lies in their being closed to the call of the Father through him. Add to that the fact that they are powerless to prevent the true flock of the Messiah coming to the shepherd and following him. The Jews are dashing themselves against the purposes of God.

The shepherd imagery that Jesus persists in using makes sense in his response to their questions – *'you are not of my sheep'* – for one of the Old Testament images of the Messiah was David, the shepherd king of Israel.

156

My sheep listen to my voice; I know them, and they follow me. I give them eternal life, and they shall never perish; no-one can snatch them out of my hand. My Father, who has given them to me, is greater than all; no-one can snatch them out of my Father's hand. I and the Father are one." 10:27-30

In concluding this exchange Jesus underlines some of the privileges enjoyed by those who are his sheep.

My sheep listen to my voice: They hear and continue to hear Christ's voice and obedience to it brings them into a new relationship with him. v. 27

I give them eternal life, and they shall never perish. They are no longer part of the passing world, under the power of the evil one, they shall never perish. *v. 28*

No-one can snatch them out of my Father's hand. (v. 29) Christ's people are his possession. In this the Father and the Son have committed themselves to keep Christ's sheep secure. (v. 30) *I and the Father are one*. Weak as we are, we shall all be saved.

Again the Jews picked up stones to stone him,
but Jesus said to them, "I have shown you many great miracles
from the Father. For which of these do you stone me?"
"We are not stoning you for any of these," replied the Jews, "but for
blasphemy, because you, a mere man, claim to be God." 10:31-32

But Jesus was not a mere man aspiring to become God. He was not *'making himself God.'* He was the incarnate God. Their eyes were blind to who Jesus was. Their hatred of him knew no bounds.

Jesus answered them, "Is it not written in your Law, 'I have said you are gods'? If he called them 'gods', to whom the word of God came—and the Scripture cannot be broken — [36]*what about the one whom the Father set apart as his very own and sent into the world?*

[36]*Why then do you accuse me of blasphemy because I said, 'I am God's Son'?* 10:34-36

If the title 'gods' was applied to the prophets, men who received the word of God, how much more appropriately is that title fitting for him who is *'the word of God '* in the flesh.

[37]*Do not believe me, unless I do what my Father does.* [38]*But if I do it, even though you do not believe me, believe the miracles that you may know and understand that the Father is in me, and I in the Father."* 10:34-38

Jesus' works / miracles carried an indelible hallmark: they were the works of God. (v. 37) The Jews were so obtuse that they refused to believe that his miracles were works of God. This is why Jesus appealed to them to *'believe the miracles.'*

[39]*Again they tried to seize him, but he escaped their grasp.* 10:39

The Jews groped for their stones, but Jesus has escaped their grasp.

Then Jesus went back across the Jordan to the place where John had been baptising in the early days. Here he stayed and many people came to him.
They said, "Though John never performed a miraculous sign, all that John said about this man was true." And in that place many believed in Jesus. 10:40-42

What a different atmosphere there is in these verses. Jesus was again among people who had respect for him. They seized the opportunity to be with him again (v. 41).

They had a conviction about Jesus in their hearts and minds, and they expressed it beautifully:

> *"Though John never performed a miraculous sign,*
> *all that John said about this man was true."*

John the Baptist's witness to Jesus bore much fruit:

> *42in that place many believed in Jesus.*

Thank You, Heavenly Father:

For the parable of the Good Shepherd; Jesus filled the position perfectly as he loved his own to the uttermost;

For Jesus' love for the lost—such as the man born blind; His love wasn't a single isolated incident in the blind man's life, it was an ongoing love until the man had life to the full.

For the confident way that Jesus could speak in advance of his resurrection—as if it were already history;

For the precious words in vv. 27 to 30, and yet there was tangible hatred in the eyes of those who heard them for the first time;

The pressure in that area was so evident that Jesus went back across Jordan, there he found some rest and relief—and fruit for his labour: *'in that place many believed in Jesus.'*

Father accept our thanks for all the wonderful things you do in and through Your Son.

In Jesus' Name, Amen.

Chapter 11

JESUS: THE RESURRECTION AND THE LIFE

THE SEVENTH SIGN:

John 11:1-16   **The death of Lazarus**

John 11: 17-37   **Jesus comforts the sisters**

John 11:38-44   **Jesus raises Lazarus from the dead**

John 11:45-57   **The Plot to kill Jesus**

If we have been observant as we made our way through the previous chapters we will know that up to chapter 10:39 Jesus had been in Jerusalem. John's footnote to that chapter reported that Jesus went back across Jordan to the place where John had been baptizing in the early days (1:28), nearly three years previously. The place was Bethabara, beyond Jordan. We are ready to move into chapter 11.

John 11:1-16

THE DEATH OF LAZARUS

Now a man named Lazarus was sick. He was from Bethany, the village of Mary and her sister Martha.
This Mary, whose brother Lazarus now lay sick, was the same one who poured perfume on the Lord and wiped his feet with her hair.
So the sisters sent word to Jesus, "Lord, the one you love is sick." 11:1-3

We get the impression that the home in Bethany, where Mary and Martha and their brother Lazarus lived, could well have been one of a number of homes, perhaps many homes where he and his disciples would receive hospitality in their itinerant ministry of preaching the gospel.

John identifies Mary as the woman who anointed Jesus' feet by pouring perfume on them and wiping his feet with her hair.

We commend the sisters for their initiative in sending for Jesus with the message 'Lord, the one you love is sick.' They didn't dictate to Jesus what they would like him to do, the simply sent their message, and waited for the Lord to do his will. They were 'a very close family' as we would say in the Ulster countryside, and they weathered crises together.

When he heard this, Jesus said, "This sickness will not end in death. No, it is for God's glory so that God's Son may be glorified through it."
Jesus loved Martha and her sister and Lazarus.

Yet when he heard that Lazarus was sick, he stayed where he was two more days. 11:4

John is careful in his recording of Jesus' actions. First he spoke some words of explanation to his disciples, teaching them that behind Lazarus' illness, there was a divine purpose. He was emphatic that *'this sickness would not end in death.'*

John, writing many years after the event, thought it necessary to inform his readers that Jesus had great affection for his three friends in Bethany.

Yet John makes no secret of the fact that Jesus seemed to delay responding to the message from the sisters, in fact he prolonged his stay beyond Jordan for a further two days!

⁷Only then did he say to his disciples: 'Let us go back to Judea.' Jesus was in Transjordan. Bethany would have been about a day's journey from there.

The disciples expressed concern for Jesus' safety.

"But Rabbi," they said, "a short while ago the Jews tried to stone you, and yet you are going back there?"
⁹Jesus answered, "Are there not twelve hours of daylight? A man who walks by day will not stumble, for he sees by this world's light.
¹⁰It is when he walks by night that he stumbles, for he has no light."
11:8-10

The disciples remembered the attempt of the Jews to kill Jesus by stoning in Jerusalem (10:31-32).

We are puzzled by the Lord's reply to the disciples in vv. 9 & 10. There is a time for travelling i.e. in daylight; travelling by night is more than ordinarily hazardous, because there is no light. Lamplight is a poor substitute for daylight.

Bishop Ryle paraphrases Jesus' reply by quoting the familiar proverb: 'Every man is immortal until his work is done.'

> [11]*After he had said this, he went on to tell them, "Our friend Lazarus has fallen asleep; but I am going there to wake him up."* [12]*His disciples replied, "Lord, if he sleeps, he will get better."*

NB: THE DISCIPLES MISUNDERSTOOD JESUS.

> [13]*Jesus had been speaking of his death, but his disciples thought he meant natural sleep.*
> [14]*So then he told them plainly, "Lazarus is dead,* [15]*and for your sake I am glad I was not there, so that you may believe. But let us go to him."* 11:11-15

NB: Even in death Lazarus is still *'our friend'*. Something more helpful for their faith is going to happen: *'I am glad I was not there, so that you may believe.'*

> *Then Thomas (called Didymus) said to the rest of the disciples, "Let us also go, that we may die with him."*
> *Thomas thought the Jesus and the disciples were walking into danger (as in v. 8), nevertheless, if martyrdom was ahead, Thomas wasn't going to back down!* 11:16

John 11: 17-37

JESUS COMFORTS THE SISTERS

¹⁷On his arrival, Jesus found that Lazarus had already been in the tomb for four days.
¹⁸Bethany was less than two miles from Jerusalem,
¹⁹and many Jews had come to Martha and Mary to comfort them in the loss of their brother.
²⁰When Martha heard that Jesus was coming, she went out to meet him, but Mary stayed at home. 11:17-20

Lazarus had been dead and four days ago he was placed in his tomb. The news of the family bereavement had spread quickly and so many Jews had come to the sisters to comfort them in the loss of their brother.

The mention of 'four days' was not without meaning. The Jews believed that by the fourth day the soul had left the corpse without any possibility of recall. In this case then, the difficulty of Lazarus being raised again seems great. His body would already have begun to decay. Any attempt to raise him could be nauseating, to say the least!

As a good pastor (shepherd) Jesus know that Martha has a lot of grief and pain and even puzzlement to unload, and so he listens carefully.

²¹"Lord," Martha said to Jesus, "if you had been here, my brother would not have died.

(This was her complaint.)

²²But I know that even now God will give you whatever you ask."

(Clearly she is not despairing, she has confidence in Jesus.)

²³Jesus said to her, "Your brother will rise again."

(Jesus gave her 'words of eternal life.') 11:21-23

Martha has been listening carefully. Her thinking is clear – her reply shows how the doctrine of the resurrection of the body gives her comfort.

²⁴Martha answered,

"I know he will rise again in the resurrection at the last day."
²⁵Jesus said to her, "I am the resurrection and the life. He who believes in me will live, even though he dies;
²⁶and whoever lives and believes in me will never die
Do you believe this?"
²⁷Yes, Lord," she told him, "I believe that you are the Christ, the Son of God, who was to come into the world." 11:24-27

See how gently Jesus led Martha onward in her faith. He brought her from resurrection at the last day, to the possibility of the resurrection in the present day. He brought her to a full-orbed faith in himself as the Messiah, the Son of God.

²⁸And after she had said this, she went back and called her sister Mary aside. "The Teacher is here," she said, "and is asking for you."
²⁹When Mary heard this, she got up quickly and went to him.
³⁰Now Jesus had not yet entered the village, but was still at the place where Martha had met him.
³¹When the Jews who had been with Mary in the house, comforting her, noticed how quickly she got up and went out, they followed her, supposing she was going to the tomb to mourn there. 11:28-31

Jesus had found the place to be somewhat private and so he waited there for Mary. She too had a load of grief and pain and complaint to unload.

> *³²When Mary reached the place where Jesus was and saw him, she fell at his feet and said, "Lord, if you had been here, my brother would not have died."*
> *³³When Jesus saw her weeping, and the Jews who had come along with her also weeping, he was deeply moved in spirit and troubled.*
> *³⁴"Where have you laid him?" he asked.*
> *"Come and see, Lord," they replied.* 11:32-34

It took fewer words to comfort Mary, but maybe Jesus was even more moved in his spirit and troubled and wept along with her.

> *³⁵Jesus wept.*
> *³⁶Then the Jews said, "See how he loved him!"*
> *But some of them said, 'Could not he who opened he eyes of the blind man have kept this man from dying.* 11:35-36

But some of them said,

> *"Could not he who opened the eyes of the blind man have kept this man from dying?"* 11:37

John 11:38-44

JESUS RAISES LAZARUS FROM THE DEAD

³⁸Jesus, once more deeply moved, came to the tomb. It was a cave with a stone laid across the entrance.
³⁹"Take away the stone," he said. "But, Lord," said Martha, the sister of the dead man, "by this time there is a bad odour, for he has been there four days."
⁴⁰Then Jesus said, "Did I not tell you that if you believed, you would see the glory of God?"
⁴¹So they took away the stone. 11:38-41

Jesus was about to proceed with the miracle of resurrection. He gave a clear instruction: 'Take away the stone.'

³⁹ᵇMartha interjected (very understandably) "But, Lord, "by this time there is a bad odour, for he has been there four days."

NB. THE BELIEF THAT THE SOUL HAD DEPARTED AFTER FOUR DAYS.

Martha's words show that she had only faint hope. Jesus corrected her troubled thoughts (probably in a quiet aside so as to cause her no embarrassment)

⁴⁰"Did I not tell you that if you believed, you would see the glory of God?"

Then Jesus prayed
⁴¹Then Jesus looked up and said, "Father, I thank you that you have heard me.

[42]I knew that you always hear me, but I said this for the benefit of the people standing here, that they may believe that you sent me."
[43]When he had said this, Jesus called in a loud voice, "Lazarus, come out!"

They said it couldn't be done – but he did it!

The dead man came out, his hands and feet wrapped with strips of linen, and a cloth around his face.
Jesus said to them, "Take off the grave clothes and let him go."
11:38-44

John 11: 45-57

THE PLOT TO KILL JESUS

Therefore many of the Jews who had come to visit Mary, and had seen what Jesus did, put their faith in him.
But some of them went to the Pharisees and told them what Jesus had done.
Then the chief priests and the Pharisees called a meeting of the Sanhedrin. "What are we accomplishing?" they asked. "Here is this man performing many miraculous signs. If we let him go on like this, everyone will believe in him, and then the Romans will come and take away both our temple and our nation. 11:45-48

The public response to the miracle was threefold: some of the Jews in the extended family of Mary and Martha and Lazarus put their faith in Jesus. Was this saving faith? It could have been: they <u>put their faith in him.</u>

Others took the shortest possible route to the Pharisees' HQ. How will they react? Like committees everywhere the Pharisees/ Official Judaism will have to 'sit on it' or 'look into the matter.'

The leadership expressed frustration over the fact that the ministry of Jesus was unstoppable. *"What are we accomplishing?" "Here is this man performing many miraculous signs."*

Their chief concern was that the Romans would not approve if the Sanhedrin (operating under Roman jurisdiction) did not take effective steps to put a stop to Jesus' ministry. The Romans might think the Sanhedrin too tolerant and take authority out of Jewish hands altogether, (in other words it would be 'direct rule').

> *If we let him go on like this, everyone will believe in him, and then the Romans will come and take away both our place and our nation."* 11:48

What did Caiaphas mean when he spoke to the Council?

> *⁴⁹Then one of them, named Caiaphas, who was high priest that year, spoke up, "You know nothing at all!*
> *⁵⁰You do not realise that it is better for you that one man die for the people than that the whole nation perish."*

NB. WHAT HE MEANT WAS 'BETTER FOR US THAT JESUS IS PUT TO DEATH THAN THAT THOUSANDS OF OUR PEOPLE DIE AT THE HANDS OF THE ROMANS SUPPRESSING A REBELLION.'

> *⁵¹He did not say this on his own, but as high priest that year he prophesied that Jesus would die for the Jewish nation, ⁵²and not only for that nation but also for the scattered children of God, to bring them together and make them one.* 11:49-53

NB. THOUGH CAIAPHAS WAS AN EVIL MAN, GOD USED HIM TO PROPHESY

This was an altogether astonishing prophesy because Caiaphas was an unwitting prophet as well as a priest. He prophesied the substitutionary death of Jesus. Jesus is to be offered up for the political salvation of Israel. But there was more in Caiaphas' words than he realised.

So from that day on they plotted to take his life. When the intentions of the Jews became known Jesus withdrew from Jerusalem.

The Romans later deposed Caiaphas and Pilate in AD 36.

Therefore Jesus no longer moved about publicly among the Jews. Instead he withdrew to a region near the desert, to a village called Ephraim, where he stayed with his disciples. 11:54

Jesus moved out of the area to a village about 12 miles north of Jerusalem. He doesn't dread the Sanhedrin, but the timing of the critical confrontation with Judaism will be in his hands, not theirs.

[55]When it was almost time for the Jewish Passover, many went up from the country to Jerusalem for their ceremonial cleansing before the Passover.
[56]They kept looking for Jesus, and as they stood in the temple area they asked one another, "What do you think? Isn't he coming to the Feast at all?"
[57]But the chief priests and Pharisees had given orders that if anyone found out where Jesus was, he should report it so that they might arrest him. 11:55-57

Jesus would die at the next Passover. As was customary Jews from all over the world would make a pilgrimage from the country and go up to Jerusalem for their ceremonial cleansing before the Passover (v. 55).

This ceremony was called Pesach. Those who had become ritually unclean because of having touched a dead body had to purify themselves by immersion (Numbers 9:10, 13).

Those who knew Jesus kept looking for him in and around the temple precincts wondering if he would come to the Passover.

Jesus was not there – at least not yet – because of the decree of the Pharisees that anyone finding Jesus should report him so that he could be arrested (v. 57).

Thank You, Heavenly Father:

For the wonder-working power of Jesus Christ in the raising of Lazarus and restoring him to his sisters;

For the gentle, understanding manner of Jesus when ministering to the grieving sisters; how he appealed to their knowledge of the scriptures and the promises of God; how he appealed to their minds as well as their hearts in order to lead them to solid comfort;

For the example of Jesus the Pastor, who alone knows human hearts.

In Jesus' Name, Amen.

Chapter 12

JOHN 12:1-11

JESUS ANOINTED AT BETHANY

Passover is drawing near and Jesus intends to be in Jerusalem, but there is time to visit his friends in Bethany.

Six days before the Passover, Jesus came to Bethany, where Lazarus lived, whom Jesus had raised from the dead.
Here a dinner was given in Jesus' honour. Martha served, while Lazarus was among those reclining at the table with him. 12:1-2

This is the final week of Jesus' life before the Cross. Jesus is the honoured guest, Lazarus is at table with the guests, and Martha is serving the food. They were all looking forward to an evening of good food and good fellowship.

Mary has not been mentioned yet. There is a reason for this.

Then Mary took about a pint of pure nard, an expensive perfume; she poured it on Jesus' feet and wiped his feet with her hair. And the house was filled with the fragrance of the perfume. 12:3

Mary performed an act of worship by anointing her Lord with perfume. She knew why. Judas didn't know why. Jesus knew why (v. 7). Judas made a hasty and harsh judgment:

> *⁴But one of his disciples, Judas Iscariot, who was later to betray him, objected, ⁵"Why wasn't this perfume sold and the money given to the poor? It was worth a year's wages."*
> *⁶He did not say this because he cared about the poor but because he was a thief; as keeper of the money bag, he used to help himself to what was put into it.* 12:4-6

So Judas' protest is recorded. So is his pilfering from the money bag. Then Jesus intervened:

> *⁷"Leave her alone," Jesus replied. "It was intended that she should save this perfume for the day of my burial.*
> *⁸You will always have the poor among you, but you will not always have me."* 12:7-8

Kindness can be shown to the living and the dead through funerals and burials whereas charity can only be shown to the living. Care for the poor is a sacred duty because it is a concern of God's own heart.

Meanwhile, what is happening outside?

> *⁹Meanwhile a large crowd of Jews found out that Jesus was there and came, not only because of him but also to see Lazarus, whom he had raised from the dead.*
> *¹⁰So the chief priests made plans to kill Lazarus as well,*
> *¹¹for on account of him many of the Jews were going over to Jesus and putting their faith in him.* 12:9-11

Notice the cost Lazarus pays for his extended life:

¹⁰So the chief priests made plans to kill Lazarus as well.

The Pharisees were helpless, unable to stop Jesus' ministry or to stop the Jewish people from putting their faith in him.

John 12:12-19

JESUS COMES TO JERUSALEM AS KING

Jesus' entry into Jerusalem is very dramatic. By openly entering the city where he is a marked man he takes a significant step towards the final confrontation with the Jews.

> *12The next day the great crowd that had come for the Feast heard that Jesus was on his way to Jerusalem.*
> *13They took palm branches and went out to meet him, shouting, "Hosanna!" "Blessed is he who comes in the name of the Lord!" "Blessed is the King of Israel!"*
> *14Jesus found a young donkey and sat upon it, as it is written, "Do not be afraid, O Daughter of Zion; see, your king is coming, seated on a donkey's colt." 12:12-15*

There are echoes here of Psalm 118:25-26 & Zechariah 9:9. We are grateful to John for pointing this out, because these connections had not occurred to the disciples. From what we know of the disciples in other situations we may surmise that they shared the nationalistic hopes of the crowd. However, Jesus really was the King of Israel.

> *At first his disciples did not understand all this. Only after Jesus was glorified did they realise that these things had been written about him and that they had done these things to him. 12:16*

176

These things had an impact on the crowd which the Jews were impotent to prevent.

This incident reaches a climax in the following verses:

[17]Now the crowd that was with him when he called Lazarus from the tomb and raised him from the dead continued to spread the word. [18]Many people, because they had heard that he had given this miraculous sign, went out to meet him.
[19]So the Pharisees said to one another, "See, this is getting us nowhere. Look how the whole world has gone after him!" 12:17-19

John 12: 20-36

JESUS PREDICTS HIS DEATH

20Now there were some Greeks among those who went up to worship at the Feast.
21They came to Philip, who was from Bethsaida in Galilee, with a request. "Sir," they said, "we would like to see Jesus."
22Philip went to tell Andrew; Andrew and Philip in turn told Jesus.
12:20-22

Something very significant was happening. These Greeks represented a Gentile nation. They wanted to speak to Jesus. The fact that they had come to worship at the feast suggests that they were proselytes to Judaism.

Jesus' reply shows that a new stage has begun in his ministry.

23Jesus replied, "The hour has come for the Son of Man to be glorified.
24I tell you the truth, unless a grain of wheat falls to the ground and dies, it remains only a single seed. But if it dies, it produces many seeds.
25The man who loves his life will lose it, while the man who hates his life in this world will keep it for eternal life.
26Whoever serves me must follow me; and where I am, my servant also will be. My Father will honour the one who serves me.
12:23-26

Jesus' first reaction is to interpret the arrival of the Greeks as an indicator of the time by God's clock. The hour of Jesus' death is very near.

Jesus' second reaction is to rejoice in the principle of harvest: death is followed by resurrection. He is like a grain of wheat. His death is like a grain of wheat being sown. It dies in the ground. Then it bursts forth into glorious harvest, in Jesus' case a harvest of souls, the travail of his soul that will give him such satisfaction (Isa. 53)

Jesus' third reaction is to lay down the harvest principle for discipleship. Lives laid down for him will be fruitful lives – even to eternal life.

Jesus' fourth reaction is to underline another principle of discipleship, following him wherever he leads.

Right there, in the midst of a great crowd of people Jesus prays aloud:

> [27]*"Now my heart is troubled, and what shall I say? 'Father, save me from this hour'? No, it was for this very reason I came to this hour.*
> [28]*Father, glorify your name!"*
> *Then a voice came from heaven, "I have glorified it, and will glorify it again." 12:27-28*

There were few who understood. We may say that none understood the closeness of Jesus and his Father.

The Son's desire: [28]*Father, glorify your name!"*

The Father's affirmation: *"I have glorified it, and will glorify it again."*

> [29]*The crowd that was there and heard it said it had thundered; others said an angel had spoken to him.*
> [30]*Jesus said, "This voice was for your benefit, not mine. 12:29-30*

He is telling them that he and they are standing at the most significant moments in human history.

> *31Now is the time for judgment on this world; now the prince of this world will be driven out.*
> *32But I, when I am lifted up from the earth, will draw all men to myself." 33He said this to show the kind of death he was going to die.*
> *34The crowd spoke up, "We have heard from the Law that the Christ will remain forever, so how can you say, 'The Son of Man must be lifted up'? Who is this 'Son of Man'?" 12:31-34*

Jesus' accomplishments on the cross will mark the defeat of the evil one (31), and the drawing together of Jesus' people from among all humanity (32).

The crowd draws on the limited knowledge that it has of the Son of Man. (they would have heard of him in the Old Testament scriptures).

They remembered that the Son of Man will reign

(e.g. Daniel 7:11-14)

'but who is THIS Son of Man?'

Jesus appears to avoid their questions at this point – he has something equally important to say:

> *35Then Jesus told them, "You are going to have the light just a little while longer. Walk while you have the light, before darkness over-takes you. The man who walks in the dark does not know where he is going.*
> *36Put your trust in the light while you have it, so that you may become sons of light."*
> *When he had finished speaking, Jesus left and hid himself from them. 12:35-36*

When Jesus turned away into the crowd and left the area he had given the people plenty to think about.

If they will put their faith in Jesus and become his disciples *(despite all their questions that for now must be unanswered)* they will be walking in the light (v. 35).
If they continue to reject him and his teaching their confusion will deepen and they will be walking in the darkness (v. 36).

John 12:37-50

BELIEF AND UNBELIEF AMONG THE JEWS

Even after Jesus had done all these miraculous signs in their presence, they still would not believe in him. 12:37

Thank God for John the Evangelist and Apostle of Jesus Christ. He has a wonderful teaching gift: always explaining anything that may not be clear to his readers / pupils. This verse is one of those comments, and if we will read on, there is a fund of information to follow (vv. 38-41).

> *38This was to fulfil the word of Isaiah the prophet:*
> *"Lord, who has believed our message and to whom has the arm of the Lord been revealed?"*
> *39For this reason they could not believe, because, as Isaiah says elsewhere:*
> *40"He has blinded their eyes and deadened their hearts, so they can neither see with their eyes, nor understand with their hearts, nor turn—and I would heal them."*
> *41Isaiah said this because he saw Jesus' glory and spoke about him.* 12:38-41

The hardness of heart found in these unbelievers is that which rejects God's mercy.

In the same place, in similar circumstances, another part of the crowd is making a different response to Jesus:

42Yet at the same time many even among the leaders believed in him. But because of the Pharisees they would not confess their faith for fear they would be put out of the synagogue;
43for they loved praise from men more than praise from God. 12:42-43

But these believers were facing another problem. They were cowards.

These people had received the revelation of the Son but were not willing to live in the light of the truth they had seen. These would-be believers are an example of the fact that faith without works is dead. They need to count the cost of becoming a disciple of Jesus—and then stand publicly on his side.

44Then Jesus cried out, "When a man believes in me, he does not believe in me only, but in the one who sent me.
45When he looks at me, he sees the one who sent me.
46I have come into the world as a light, so that no-one who believes in me should stay in darkness. 12:44-46

To believe in Jesus means that we believe in the Father also (v. 44).

To know Jesus is to know the Father (v. 45).

To know Jesus is to walk in the light and not in darkness. (V. 46)

47"As for the person who hears my words but does not keep them, I do not judge him. For I did not come to judge the world, but to save it.
48There is a judge for the one who rejects me and does not accept my words; that very word which I spoke will condemn him at the last day.
49For I did not speak of my own accord, but the Father who sent me commanded me what to say and how to say it.

[50]I know that his command leads to eternal life. So whatever I say is just what the Father has told me to say." 12:47-50

To reject Jesus' words is to reject Jesus himself. The message such rejecters heard will be their judge on the last day. The word that would have saved will then condemn.

Christ's words are utterly dependable because they carry the imprimatur of the God the Father (vv 49–50).

Thank You, Heavenly Father:

For the fact that the children of Jerusalem and many in the crowds recognised Jesus because he rode into Jerusalem as the prophets had predicted;

For the joy of Jesus when Andrew and Philip introduced the Greeks to him; He saw in them the first-fruits of his personal harvest;

For yet another instance in which Jesus is battling with the unbelief of the Jews; he could not have revealed himself more fully, nor spoken more clearly yet they continued in unbelief; at the same time there were those who believed in him, but did not witness to the fact publicly because they loved the praise of men more than the praise of God;

In Jesus' Name, Amen.

A few comments about John chapters 13 to 21

I f you are reading this page it should mean that you success-fully navigated your way through John chapters 1 to 12.

The early chapters were so full of material that you may well have been grateful for the shorter sections that were suggested.

Chapters 13 to 21 are about Jesus' ministry to his disciples.

The crowds that followed Jesus are not entirely absent from the narrative. Jesus' primary task in those days was the preparation of his disciples for his absence. This was absolutely essential because he had so much still to teach them, and yet the time remaining to him was 'flying'.

Please take the opportunity to meditate on the experiences of Jesus – as well as those of his disciples.

Only heaven knows the demands that his last days on earth made on him in the period before the Cross and then again before his ascension to heaven.

I know that you will treasure many of Jesus' words in these chapters. It was clearly a labour of love for the aged apostle John to place the words and works of his beloved Lord and Saviour on record.

His ministry was especially for his disciples, and we will not have gone far in the Acts of the Apostles until we are able to trace the benefits that they reaped from his teaching.

May the Holy Spirit be your teacher,
and may your heart be strangely warmed
as you read the Gospel of John.

Chapter 13

In the opening 12 chapters of this gospel the focus was on the public ministry of Jesus. Now the focus changes and He gives almost all His attention to the needs of His disciples.

John 13: 1-17

JESUS WASHES HIS DISCIPLES' FEET

The section begins with an historical marker: 13:1

It was just before the Passover Feast. Jesus knew that the time had come for him to leave this world and go to the Father.

Jesus had a special and personal reason for wanting to eat this Passover with His disciples (Luke 22:14-16).

First of all, it was the last Passover He would ever attend;

Secondly, He knew that this Passover coincided with His offering himself as the Lamb of God's appointing on the cross at Calvary;

Thirdly, the next time He would celebrate with His disciples would be in the kingdom of God (Luke 22:16 & 18). That will not be a Passover in the tradition of the Jews, but the Marriage Supper of the Lamb (Rev.19:6-9).

Fourthly, He knew that 'His hour' had come. He would soon be returning to the glory which He had with His Father from before the foundation of the world.

There was so much more teaching that He had to share with His disciples – and there was so little time left – much less than 24 hours! If we are correct in thinking of this event taking place in the Upper Room in Jerusalem on the day before Passover, then it is already Thursday of Passover Week (or Passion Week). To-morrow He will be crucified and will die on the Cross!

Having loved his own disciples who were in the world, he now showed them the full extent of his love. 13:1

His love for them filled His every waking moment. Witness: – this sentence.

We ask ourselves: *'What does this sentence mean?'*

A tour of Bible versions helps to clarify the meaning.

NIV   he now showed them *the full extent of his love*.

KJV   he loved them *unto the end*

(Anon.)   he now *loved them to the uttermost*

HSB   he loved them *completely and always*

The Message having loved his dear companions, *he continued to love them right to the end*.

Amp Bible as he had loved those who were His own in the world *He loved them to the last and to the highest degree*.

J McArthur   *with perfect, saving, eternal love*

J.B. Phil   *from the very first day to the very last day*

Comm.   *He loved them to the limit*

A summary of the information provided by the various Bible versions and commentaries amounts to this:-*'In the whole range of Christ's contact with his disciples he loved them.'*

We wonder how often the disciples thought of their relationship with their Master in terms of *His 'loving' them.*

The disciples will soon be denied their Master's physical presence with them in the world, therefore he gives them His undivided attention.

The next 40 days or so will make big changes to their world and to *their 'in the flesh'* relationship with Jesus, because He will soon return to the Father (v. 1). He demonstrated His love in a not-to-be-forgotten way!

THE SETTING WAS A MEAL SHARED WITH HIS DISICPLES

13:2   *The evening meal was being served.*

13:2   *The devil had already prompted Judas Iscariot, son of Simon, to betray Jesus.*

13:3   *Jesus knew that the Father had put all things under his power, and that he had come from God and was returning to God;*

v. 2   seems to hint that this will be a bitter-sweet evening.

v. 3   assures us that Jesus had perfect knowledge and complete control of all the factors in the room.

So far as He was concerned He was walking in harmony with the will of His Father in heaven, as He had been doing all His life.

THE ACTION OF JESUS WAS UNPRECEDENTED

So he got up from the meal, took off his outer clothing, and wrapped a towel round his waist. After that, he poured water into a basin and began to wash his disciples' feet, drying them with the towel that was wrapped round him. 13:4-5

Jesus took a common courtesy (*'foot-washing'*) which his disciples had neglected to perform, and taught them a memorable lesson about loving one another.

It was customary for guests attending meals in the East to be shown the courtesy of having their feet washed, to get rid of the dust of the street and to refresh them generally.

This task was performed by a slave – certainly not by the Host.

The disciples gathered at the table were prepared to partake of the meal with their feet unwashed – none of them contemplated washing each other's feet.

To their surprise,

Jesus got up from the meal, took of His outer garment, wrapped a towel around His waist, poured water into a basin and began to wash the disciples' feet, drying them with the towel that was wrapped around Him. 13:4

PETER COMPLETELY MISUNDERSTOOD THE ACTION OF JESUS

He came to Simon Peter, who said to him, "Lord, are you going to wash my feet?"

Jesus replied, "You do not realise now what I am doing, but later you will understand."
"No," said Peter, "you shall never wash my feet." Jesus answered, "Unless I wash you, you have no part with me."
"Then, Lord," Simon Peter replied, "not just my feet, but my hands and my head as well!"
Jesus answered, "A person who has had a bath needs only to wash his feet; his whole body is clean. And you are clean, though not every one of you."
For he knew who was going to betray him, and that was why he said not everyone was clean. 13:6-11

We follow the exchange between Jesus and Peter and begin to realise that this is not merely the common courtesy of foot-washing that Jesus is extending to His guests, there is ministry here too.

What is happening is an acted parable about the personal relationship of Jesus and Peter (and the other disciples).

Most guests would have bathed before leaving home, therefore on arrival at the home of their host, they needed only to have their feet washed.

There is a lesson here about maintaining a clean relationship with Jesus on a daily basis.

Jesus has cleansed each of His people from sin, and so they are clean; but on a daily basis they need *'a foot-washing'*. Jesus distinguished between an over-all cleansing *(having a bath)* and a 'foot-washing' *(i.e. daily ablutions and hygiene)*

We must not miss Jesus' reply to Peter in v. 7,

"You do not realise now what I am doing,
but later you will understand."

Peter missed the point. Jesus was looking ahead to the cross and His cleansing sacrifice for sin that He would offer there. It is only with hindsight that we realise that this was His viewpoint.

JESUS EXPLAINED HIS ACTION

When he had finished washing their feet, he put on his clothes and returned to his place. "Do you understand what I have done for you?" he asked them.
"You call me 'Teacher' and 'Lord', and rightly so, for that is what I am.
Now that I, your Lord and Teacher, have washed your feet, you also should wash one another's feet.
I have set you an example that you should do as I have done for you.
I tell you the truth, no servant is greater than his master, nor is a messenger greater than the one who sent him.
Now that you know these things, you will be blessed if you do them.
13:12-17

Numerous commentators point out that the disciples called Jesus 'Lord' and 'Teacher' or 'Master' and never by His name Jesus. Some of these strongly insist that we should imitate the disciples in this.

'Lord', 'Teacher', 'Master' are appropriate and adequate and respectful names for the one whom His parents named JESUS.

JESUS WASHED JUDAS' FEET

Judas was one of those who sat at table sharing the meal and so was one of those whose feet were washed by Jesus. His heart, however, was elsewhere.

What is the spiritual condition of those who sit in our churches, professing to be believers, perhaps are in membership, whose hearts are in darkness, like Judas?

The safety of everyone who professes the name of Christ lies in keeping close to Him and living in the light of His word.

THE EXAMPLE THAT JESUS GAVE HIS DISCIPLES

"You call me 'Teacher' and 'Lord', and rightly so, for that is what I am. Now that I, your Lord and Teacher, have washed your feet, you also should wash one another's feet. I have set you an example that you should do as I have done to you.' 13:13:14)

Jesus did not deny these names that were commonly used by the disciples – but did they realise the meaning of those names: *'Teacher'* and *'Lord'*?

Eventually, when face-to-face with the Risen Lord, Thomas would address Jesus without hesitation as *'My Lord and my God'*. 20:28

Here in (13:14) the greater the title Jesus uses, the greater the challenge of His action.

Humility is a universal Christian virtue to be expressed through sincere and costly service to others in Christ's name.

Christian churches and fellowships are possible only where this attitude is expressed. If Jesus stooped in humility to minister to His disciples, how much more ought we to be ready to serve even the least and meanest of His followers.

If Jesus is our *'Teacher'* then our minds must be submissive to his words, his standards, values, attitudes, commandments, example and teaching so that these rule our thoughts and determine our convictions.

If Jesus is not our *'Teacher'* He is not our *'Lord'*.

DON'T MISS THE BENEDICTION OF JESUS.

'Now that you know these things, you will be blessed if you do them.' 13:17

Perhaps a word of explanation is needed here. Believe it or not, there are various denominations that practice foot-washing. They believe that Jesus meant his church to incorporate this in their worship. That is one point of view.

Foot-washing is not an ordinance of Christ's church. It is not enjoined anywhere else in the New Testament.

Another point of view, which I believe is the correct one, is that Jesus used a local custom in the Middle East, i.e. foot-washing, a courtesy shown to guests arriving at your home after walking dusty roads to get to your address because it suited his teaching purpose, as an illustration of humble service to his disciples.

Ch. 13:17 does not mean that we shall experience new blessings from our Lord if we take up the custom of foot-washing. It means that if we serve one another in the spirit of Jesus manifested in what he did that day to his disciples then we shall be blessed in the seeking one another's welfare with renewed enthusiasm.

John 13:18-30

JESUS PREDICTS HIS BETRAYAL

"I am not referring to all of you; I know those I have chosen. But this is to fulfil the scripture: 'He who shares my bread has lifted up his heel against me.' (Psalm 41:9)
"I am telling you now before it happens, so that when it does happen you will believe that I am He.
I tell you the truth, whoever accepts anyone I send accepts me; and whoever accepts me accepts the one who sent me."
After he had said this, Jesus was troubled in spirit and testified, "I tell you the truth, one of you is going to betray me." 13:18-21

Please note some factors with regard to Jesus and Judas.

1. **Judas' betrayal did not come as a surprise to Jesus. Nevertheless** He was deeply affected by it (v. 18).

2. **Jesus knew that Judas was going to betray Him, yet He related to that disciple with gracious words and actions.**

3. **Jesus didn't view Satan's actions with cool detachment.** He hated the destruction worked by Satan in human lives. *'Jesus was troubled in spirit.'*

Jesus was troubled by the desecration of the Temple (2:13-17); He was troubled by the sorrow of Mary at the death of her brother Lazarus (11:33); here he is troubled by the fact that the Devil had desecrated another temple, this time the life of His disciple Judas.

His disciples stared at one another, at a loss to know which of them he meant. One of them, the disciple whom Jesus loved, was reclining next to him.
Simon Peter motioned to this disciple and said, "Ask him which one he means." Leaning back against Jesus, he asked him, "Lord, who is it?"
Jesus answered, "It is the one to whom I will give this piece of bread when I have dipped it in the dish." Then, dipping the piece of bread, he gave it to Judas Iscariot, son of Simon

It was a sign of special favour when the host at a meal made the gift of a tit-bit to one of the guests. Judas knew the significance of the tit-bit.

As soon as Judas took the bread, Satan entered into him. "What you are about to do, do quickly," Jesus told him, 13:22-27

In accepting this token of favour Judas persisted in his fateful choice to betray Jesus, and sell himself to the powers of darkness. (v. 26)

When Judas left the gathering the other disciples did not know the reason for his departure. Judas' defection was a complete surprise to them.

Since Judas had charge of the money, some thought Jesus was telling him to buy what was needed for the Feast, or to give something to the poor. As soon as Judas had taken the bread, he went out. And it was night.13:29-30

In the minds of some this may raise the question of a maintaining a 'pure membership' in a local church. The most experienced pastors and evangelists will be the first to say *'Only*

Christ knows the hearts of professing believers. The matter will be clarified at the last day.'

On the other hand those who are observant will remark: *'There is a road to hell from the gates of heaven.'*

John 13:31-38

JESUS PREDICTS PETER'S DENIAL

³¹When he (Judas) was gone, Jesus said, "Now is the Son of Man glorified and God is glorified in him. ³²If God is glorified in him, God will glorify the Son in himself, and will glorify him at once. ³³"My children, I will be with you only a little longer. You will look for me, and just as I told the Jews, so I tell you now: Where I am going, you cannot come.

³⁴"A new command I give you: Love one another. As I have loved you, so you must love one another. ³⁵By this all men will know that you are my disciples, if you love one another." 13:31-35

Jesus has admitted the disciples to His knowledge of the immediate future. He has fed them this information on a need-to-know basis, otherwise they will be a very confused group of men. The words that gripped Peter were *'Where I am going, you cannot come.' v* 33

This was important and essential information – but what Jesus said next was equally significant: "A new command I give you: Love one another. As I have loved you, so you must love one another.

By this all men will know that you are my disciples, if you love one another."

Jesus is preparing the disciples for their post-Easter work – the work of world-evangelisation, no less! Part of their witness before the watching world will be their love for one another.

Their love for their Teacher and Lord must be total, and must be accompanied by an evident love for one another.

We might say: this is the *'double-whammy'*

the world has yet to receive from the Christian Church

So, you see, what we pointed out at the beginning of this study was correct: Jesus took a common courtesy ('foot-washing') which his disciples had neglected to perform, and taught them a memorable lesson about loving one another.

We cannot stop here, because John has not yet put down his quill. Read on.

> [36]*Simon Peter asked him, "Lord, where are you going?"*
> *Jesus replied, "Where I am going, you cannot follow now, but you will follow later."*
> [37]*Peter asked, "Lord, why can't I follow you now? I will lay down my life for you."*
> [38]*Then Jesus answered, "Will you really lay down your life for me? I tell you the truth, before the cock crows, you will disown me three times! 13:36-38*

Jesus knew that Peter would deny Him, yet He did not withhold the painful truth from that disciple. He spoke the truth to Peter – in love.

In spite of all that Jesus had spoken about His suffering and death, His burial and resurrection, Peter was sadly deficient in understanding the mission of his Master.

'Love is patient, love is kind'.   The Apostle Paul (1 Cor. 13:4)

'Love is kind, and suffers long' Christopher Wordsworth

Thank You, Heavenly Father:

For the facility of confessing our sins to you, and receiving for-giveness from Your hand, for Jesus sake. We feel ashamed when we think of how often we grieved our Lord and Master, when like Peter, we did not understand his perfect will;

For the humility of Jesus in his action of washing the feet of his disciples; he did not stand on ceremony, but humbly and honestly showed how much he cared for each and all of them;

That the major reason why we love You is because You first loved us;

For that beautiful expression in John 13:1 where it is written of Jesus *'Having love his own, he loved them to the end.'* We understand this expression means that *'he loved us to the uttermost.'* Heavenly Father, shed that love abroad in our hearts.

In Jesus' Name, Amen.

Chapter 14

We are in a slight difficulty here because we have fallen into the trap of having two outlines in this chapter. The NIV-UK version outlines it as shown above.

However once we get into the chapter we discover that Jesus will be answering a series of question that were put to him by his men. These introduce another outline. It so happened that it was convenient to show the existence of the two outlines on the same plan.

John 14: 1-4

JESUS COMFORTS HIS DISCIPLES

There were troubled hearts in the group of disciples at the close of chapter 13. They had witnessed the defection of Judas, heard Peter being warned by Jesus about denying his Master three times before dawn would break the following morning. Recall Jesus' words.

"Will you really lay down your life for me? I tell you the truth, before the cock crows, you will disown me three times! 13:38

Peter must have been stunned, when despite his protestations of loyalty he heard Jesus speaking the truth to him in love.

Before chapter 14 ends we shall hear Jesus answering questions that were troubling **Peter** (vv 1-4), **Thomas** (vv 5-7), **Philip** (vv 8-21) and **Jude** – not Iscariot (vv 22-31).

WHY WERE THE DISCIPLES TROUBLED AND ANXIOUS?

At least two reasons are in the closing verses of chapter 13.

1st **John 13:33. Jesus was going away.**

"My children, I will be with you only a little longer. You will look for me, and just as I told the Jews, so I tell you now: Where I am going, you cannot come.

Despite Jesus' repeated attempts to prepare them for the forthcoming separation, their hearts were filled with sorrow. The disciples felt as if they were losing a parent and being left as orphans (14:18).

2nd John 13:38. Jesus' foretelling Peter's denials must have shaken the disciples to their roots. If Peter will do such a thing–will they prove any stronger in their loyalty to Jesus? Jesus understood their thoughts and immediately ministered to them. He wants their troubled minds to be at peace.

(HERE FOLLOWS THE SECOND OUTLINE.)
JESUS ANSWERS PETER vv. 1-4

"Do not let your hearts be troubled. Trust in God; trust also in me. In my Father's house are many rooms; if it were not so, I would have told you. I am going there to prepare a place for you. And if I go and prepare a place for you, I will come back and take you to be with me that you also may be where I am. You know the way to the place where I am going." 14:1-4

If Peter will concentrate on what Jesus is saying now, he will have his questions answered in full. Although Jesus' own heart was troubled in 13:21 (by the defection of Judas) he tells his disciples that they need not be troubled at all, if they will trust the Father and trust Him.

"Do not let your hearts be troubled. Trust in God; trust also in me.

Are you listening, Peter? Here is the answer to where Jesus is going.

In my Father's house are many rooms; if it were not so, I would have told you.

There's more, Peter. Listen! Why is He going there?

I am going there to prepare a place for you. And if I go and prepare a place for you, I will come back and take you to be with me that you also may be where I am.

In using terminology like this
Jesus was drawing on their knowledge of Him.

What does all this information tell you, Peter?

It means that Jesus will continue in the fullness of His life, but in a different place. Jesus called that place 'My Father's house'.

It means that if Jesus does not leave them and go to His Father's house then rooms will not be prepared for them in God's eternal home.

It means that having prepared your rooms He will come back (at an undisclosed time in the future) and take you to be with Him where He is.

Jesus is referring to His coming again, His glorious appearing at the end of the ages, *His Parousia*. Although centuries have passed since this promise was made, its fulfilment is certain. The Lord is coming to take His people home to share His glory (17:24).

Notice that Jesus didn't elaborate on the future state of believers. Basically, *'we shall be where Jesus is!* The old gospel hymn expressed this in a memorable line: *'Where Jesus is, 'tis heaven there!'*

Peter, what was the last thing that Jesus said?

You know the way to the place where I am going."

Where has He gone? To His Father's house. There was no other answer at that point.

There are things we do not fully know, but we know that the assurance of eternal life with Jesus in His heavenly home is possible only because He goes away from us through His cross, resurrection and ascension.

Our troubled hearts will find rest in the confidence that Jesus is coming again as He promised, and that He has prepared a place for all who love Him in the glory that will surely be.

JESUS ANSWERS THOMAS vv. 5-7

Thomas said to him, "Lord, we don't know where you are going, so how can we know the way?"
Jesus answered, "I am the way and the truth and the life. No-one comes to the Father except through me.
If you really knew me, you would know my Father as well. From now on, you do know him and have seen him." 14:5-7

I suspect that if Thomas hadn't voiced the question in v. 5 – then Peter would have asked it.

[5] Thomas said to him, "Lord, we don't know where you are going, so how can we know the way?"

Thomas, are you listening carefully? Jesus is about to give you a very helpful clue about where He has gone.

*⁶Jesus answered, "I am the way and the truth and the life.
No-one comes to the Father except through me.*

Thomas, Jesus is going to be with His Father. How can we know the way?

Jesus is the way, the only way to the Father. He is our mediator. We approach God the Father through His Son Jesus. The way to the Father is Jesus Himself. He is also the Truth and the Life. From Him all revelation comes and in Him is eternal life found.

The exclusiveness of Christ's salvation is explained by the uniqueness of his divine person.

JESUS ANSWERS PHILIP vv. 8-21

*Philip said, "Lord, show us the Father and that will be enough
for us."
Jesus answered: "Don't you know me, Philip, even after I have
been among you such a long time?
Anyone who has seen me has seen the Father. How can you say,
'Show us the Father'? 14:8-9*

Philip, I'm glad you asked that question, because I'm sure that some of the other disciples are grateful that you did.

Philip said, "Lord, show us the Father and that will be enough for us."

Philip, am I right in thinking that I can hear Jesus heave a sigh?

How discouraging for Jesus, to be faced in these final moments of his instruction with this particular request, reflecting such ignorance of the Father!

The words I say to you are not just my own. Rather, it is the Father, living in me, who is doing his work.
Believe me when I say that I am in the Father and the Father is in me; or at least believe on the evidence of the miracles themselves. Don't you believe that I am in the Father, and that the Father is in me? 14:10-11

This statement is a wonderful description of the complete unity between Jesus and the Father.

The words and works of Jesus are the words and works of the Father in Him. No other explanation of them is possible.

I tell you the truth, anyone who has faith in me will do what I have been doing. He will do even greater things than these, because I am going to the Father.
And I will do whatever you ask in my name, so that the Son may bring glory to the Father. You may ask me for anything in my name, and I will do it. 14:12-14

Jesus works of preaching, teaching and healing were confined to the land of Judea and Samaria. The greater work must mean the preaching of the gospel throughout the world *'in Jerusalem, Judea and Samaria and to the ends of the earth.'* *'Greater works'* must mean more conversions. There is no greater work possible than the conversion of a soul. The powers of the kingdom are available only through believing prayer in Jesus name (vv 13-14). The outcome will be the glory of the Father through Jesus the Son.

John 14:15-31

JESUS PROMISES THE HOLY SPIRIT

The second major part of the chapter begins here.

"If you love me, you will obey what I command.
And I will ask the Father, and he will give you another Counsellor
to be with you for ever— the Spirit of truth. The world cannot
accept him, because it neither sees him nor knows him. But you
know him, for he lives with you and will be in you.
I will not leave you as orphans; I will come to you.
Before long, the world will not see me any more, but you will see
me. Because I live, you also will live.
On that day you will realise that I am in my Father, and you are in
me, and I am in you.
Whoever has my commands and obeys them, he is the one who
loves me. He who loves me will be loved by my Father, and I too
will love him and show myself to him." 14:15-21

Jesus wasn't just answering the questions of Peter, Thomas and Philip.

All the disciples were listening and learning. Here is some more good news – again it is dependent on Jesus' going away – the advent of the Holy Spirit.

Jesus' teaching is providing clear principles and precepts for his disciples to live by.

John 13:34   "A new command I give you: Love one another.

John 14:1   "Do not let your hearts be troubled. Trust in God; trust also in me.

John 14:11   Believe me when I say that I am in the Father and the Father is in me.

John 14:15   "If you love me, you will obey what I command.

Jesus' departure and exaltation in heaven will secure the ministry of the Holy Spirit.

And I will ask the Father, and he will give you another Counsellor to be with you for ever— the Spirit of truth. The world cannot accept him, because it neither sees him nor knows him. But you know him, for he lives with you and will be in you. 14:16-17

This Counsellor is the Spirit of truth.

This Counsellor is a person.

This Counsellor will come to those who know him.

This Counsellor will live in the disciples.

Jesus called the Counsellor *'the parakletos'* –

'one called alongside to help.'

I will not leave you as orphans; I will come to you.

John 14:18

Jesus will be leaving them. The Holy Spirit, *'Christ's Other Self'* will be with them. This will bring about an intimacy and a union that is utterly unique in relationships:

Before long, the world will not see me any more, but you will see me. Because I live, you also will live. On that day you will realise that I am in my Father, and you are in me, and I am in you.
Whoever has my commands and obeys them, he is the one who loves me. He who loves me will be loved by my Father, and I too will love him and show myself to him."
Then Judas (not Judas Iscariot) said, "But, Lord, why do you intend to show yourself to us and not to the world?" 14:19-22

The answer to Judas' question is given at length in the following verses: but in short it is simply this: *the disciples know Him and the world does not!*

In vv. 23 & 24 the emphasis is on 'if anyone loves me.'

Jesus replied, "If anyone loves me, he will obey my teaching. My Father will love him, and we will come to him and make our home with him. He who does not love me will not obey my teaching. These words you hear are not my own; they belong to the Father who sent me. 14:23-24

Jesus has more to say to them about the Holy Spirit.

"All this I have spoken while still with you. But the Counsellor, the Holy Spirit, whom the Father will send in my name, will teach you all things and will remind you of everything I have said to you. Peace I leave with you; my peace I give you. I do not give to you as the world gives. Do not let your hearts be troubled and do not be afraid. 14:25-27

The Holy Spirit will be sent to them by the Father in the name of the Son.

The Holy Spirit will be their Teacher (instructing them further).

The Holy Spirit will keep their Master's teaching before their minds.

Some of these men would go on to write various books of the New Testament, a task that would require the ministry of the Holy Spirit in abundant measure.

Jesus brings them back to the 'painful' subject of His going away in order to help them look on it with 'gladness'.

*"You heard me say, 'I am going away and I am coming back to you.'
If you loved me, you would be glad that I am going to the Father,
for the Father is greater than I.*

The teaching He had given them has prepared them for His leaving.

*I have told you now before it happens so that when it does happen
you will believe.* 14:28-31

Time is getting short—only He knows how short, it can now be counted in hours and not days—when the Devil will make a final assault on Jesus the Son of God.

*I will not speak with you much longer, for the prince of this world
is coming. He has no hold on me, but the world must learn that
I love the Father and that I do exactly what my Father has commanded me.* 14:31

Jesus would go to the cross and sacrifice Himself because He loved His Father and gave total obedience to His commands. *'He became obedient to death—even death on a cross!* (Phil. 2:9)
"Come now; let us leave.

At this point the whole group left the Upper Room to make their way across the city to the Garden of Gethsemane. Chapters 15 to 17 record Jesus' conversation on His last journey.

Thank You, Heavenly Father:

For the heart to heart conversation that Jesus had with his
  disciples, despite the heavy pressures that were gathering
  around him;

For the patient way in which he answered the various concerns
of his disciples;

For the adequate preparation for the future changes in all their
lives that he conveyed to them in an impromptu way; yet he
was giving them total care;

In Jesus' Name

Chapter 15:

Whether all that is recorded in John chapters 15 -17 was spoken in the Upper Room at Jerusalem is a matter of opinion. Commentators on the Gospels differ. Martin Luther is reported to have said: *'When the angels want a good laugh, they read the commentaries.'*

In John's gospel, Jesus' words in 14:31 mark a cut-off point in the narrative and the location. *'Come now, let us leave'* He said, indicating that all that follows was spoken as He and the disciples walked to the Garden of Gethsemane.

We can imagine them walking through the darkened streets of the city and then passing beyond the walls into the sur-rounding countryside.

As they walked, Jesus began to talk to them about vines, vine dressers and fruit. What prompted him to do this? In addi-tion to the initiative of Jesus there are several possibilities.

(1) Something they saw may have prompted the subject. No doubt they would have passed near the temple which had great vines carved into its doors. They may have passed through the Golden Gate which also had gorgeous vines carved into it. Of course, it was April, and that meant that

the grape vines would be beginning to blossom with the promise of a fresh harvest.

(2) Jesus' reason may have been much more profound. The biblical symbol for Israel was a vine.

You brought a vine out of Egypt; you drove out the nations and planted it. You cleared the ground for it, and it took root and filled the land. The mountains were covered with its shade, the mighty cedars with its branches. (Psalm 80:8-10)
I will sing for the one I love a song about his vineyard: My loved one had a vineyard on a fertile hillside. He dug it up and cleared it of stones and planted it with the choicest vines. He built a watch-tower in it and cut out a winepress as well. Then he looked for a crop of good grapes, but it yielded only bad fruit. Isa. 5:1-2

But, this vine had not lived up to its intended purpose.

I had planted you like a choice vine of sound and reliable stock. How then did you turn against me into a corrupt, wild vine? Although you wash yourself with soda and use an abundance of soap, the stain of your guilt is still before me," declares the Sovereign LORD. Jer. 2:21
Israel was a spreading vine; he brought forth fruit for himself. As his fruit increased, he built more altars; as his land prospered, he adorned his sacred stones. Hosea 10:1

Therefore, God had sent His Son into this world as *"The True Vine"*.

The nation of Israel symbolised by the vine, had grown wild, but Jesus had been obedient to the will of His Father.

What Israel had failed to do, He would accomplish!

Whatever prompted this teaching that night it is clear that His desire was to teach them about the most vital relationship in their lives, the one with Jesus and His Father. We might ask ourselves *"Why did Jesus give them this teaching now?"* The answer is simple: They needed it!

These men have just been informed that Jesus is going away, but that His work is going to continue, and that it is to continue through them and their lives. If they were to carry on the work of the Lord, then they needed to know how to produce that kind of fruit in their lives.

He wants them to know that the only way they can be fruitful for the glory of God is to abide in Him, the True Vine.

Jesus had spoken of
the cleansing of the disciples (13:10-11),
the coming intimacy with Him and His Father (14:20-21),
the coming of the Holy Spirit (14:16-17, 26),
and the command to love one another (13:34-35).
All these themes, among others, crop up again
in Jesus' teaching of the vine and its branches (15:1-17).

NB. I have made a point of avoiding big words and lengthy headings so that the newest believer among us may have minimum difficulty in grasping the lessons that Jesus was teaching the disciples.
The 'headings' such as they are, are set out as declarations that Jesus made as he unfolded his teaching to his men.
There is also provision for a long pause in the middle so that there is no need to rush on merely for the sake of completing another chapter.

John 15–Part One

THE VINE AND THE BRANCHES 15:1-17

Jesus declares that he is the true vine and his father is the gardener

"I am the true vine, and my Father is the gardener. 15:1

Jesus is taking the biblical image of Israel and applying it to Himself. Israel's place as the people of God is now taken by Jesus and His disciples, the vine and its branches. Israel as the Vine of God planted in the Promised Land is now replaced by Jesus, and the people of God are no longer associated with a territory. In time they will become international as in Acts 1:8

> *But you will receive power when the Holy Spirit comes on you; and you will be my witnesses in Jerusalem, and in all Judea and Samaria, and to the ends of the earth."* Acts 1:8

Jesus is the TRUE VINE in contrast to the Jewish Leaders (Official Israel) who have rejected Him and thus cut themselves off from Him and His Father.

Jesus declares that he is the vine and believers are the branches

The role of His Father as the GARDENER continues the theme of Jesus' dependence on and subordination to His Father.

He cuts off every branch in me that bears no fruit, while every branch that does bear fruit he prunes so that it will be even more fruitful. 15:2

Jesus declares that his Father the Gardener carries out two tasks so that the branches are maintained in a healthy and fruitful condition – they are known as CUTTING OFF and CUTTING BACK.

He does these two things to ensure that there will be as much fruit as possible–in the winter he *cuts off* the dry and withered branches and in the spring he removes the rank and useless growths from the branches *cutting back* surplus shoots that would hinder the vine's development *so that it will be even more fruitful.*

Jesus speaks about cleanliness v. 3

Recall Jesus' words to Peter at the foot-washing: *Jesus answered, "A person who has had a bath needs only to wash his feet; his whole body is clean. And you are clean, though not every one of you."* 13:10

Jesus is repeating what He had said at the foot-washing. Hence v. 3. *You are already clean* because of the word I have spoken to you.

So far Jesus has taught that the Father prunes and cleanses, and the Son cleanses by His word. The Father and the Son are at one in this work.

Jesus speaks next about fruitfulness vv. 4-6

Jesus stresses the impossibility of producing fruit apart from him!

Fruit-bearing for God is a human impossibility!

Fruit-bearing for God is the work of Christ in us.

The disciples may still have much in their lives that is not in keeping with the life of God. Such false growths need to be pruned away so that His eternal life might grow and increase in their lives.

Jesus speaks about living in him vv. 4-6

> *"Remain in me, and I will remain in you. No branch can bear fruit by itself; it must remain in the vine. Neither can you bear fruit unless you remain in me.*
> *I am the vine; you are the branches. If a man remains in me and I in him, he will bear much fruit; apart from me you can do nothing. If anyone does not remain in me, he is like a branch that is thrown away and withers; such branches are picked up, thrown into the fire and burned.* John 15:4-6

The KJV uses the word *'abide'*, the NIV and some other versions use the word *'remain'*. Some paraphrases use the word *'live'*. This third word is very helpful. Try it in verses 4–6 and listen to it!

v. 4 "LIVE in me, and I will LIVE in you.

No branch can bear fruit by itself; it must LIVE in the vine. Neither can you bear fruit unless you LIVE in me.

v. 5 I am the vine; you are the branches.

If a man remains/LIVES in me and I (LIVE) in him, he will bear much fruit; apart from me you can do nothing.

v. 6 if anyone does not remain/LIVE in me, he is like a branch that is thrown away and withers; such branches are picked up, thrown into the fire and burned.

The alternatives are starkly expressed.

The consequence of LIVING IN HIM is the bearing of much fruit (v. 5).

The consequence of NOT LIVING IN HIM is being cast out, withered, gathered and burned (v. 6).

Jesus stresses the impossibility of producing fruit apart from him!

He is also stressing that

no one can be a branch in him

and a member of his body,

who does not bear fruit.

Here follows a long pause:

Take as long as you need to make your way through this section.

I HAVE INSERTED IT BECAUSE IT CANNOT BE ASSUMED

THAT ALL MY READERS ARE AT THE SAME STAGE

OF SPIRITUAL GROWTH.

HOW SHALL WE UNDERSTAND
THIS TEACHING OF JESUS?

Drawing on our wider knowledge of the Scriptures some matters can be clarified. One thing we know for sure: He is not contradicting Himself.

We can go from Scripture to Scripture and find help. – somewhat as follows

1. *If any man be in Christ, he is a new creation* (2 Cor. 5:17)
   This means that every branch in the True Vine is a true believer, regenerated by the Holy Spirit.

Only true believers can be said to be *'in Christ'*.

Whatever people may profess to be, or appear to be, *it is impossible for an unregenerate person to be 'in Christ', to be a branch in the True Vine.*

2. This means that the references to the work of the Father (the Gardener), describe His necessary work of **cutting off** and **cutting back** the branches, to improve the fruitfulness of the living branches in the True Vine.

3. *If anyone does not remain in me, he is like a branch that is thrown away and withers; such branches are picked up, thrown into the fire and burned.*

Can we think of instances where believers were *'cut off'*, when the Lord disciplined them for their wrongdoing?

Yes, we can.

Acts 5. Ananias and Sapphira *'lied to the Holy Spirit'* about the price they received for a plot of land. *They paid for their sin with their lives!*

1 Cor. 11:23ff In the church there was serious disorder in the observance of the Lord's Supper. Did the Lord ignore their behaviour?

No, He didn't.

1 Cor. 11: 30 *'This is why many among you are weak and sick, and a number of you have fallen asleep.' i.e. have died.*

In Revelation 2 & 3 there are seven letters from the Risen Lord to the seven churches in Asia. They are compared to lamp-stands.

Notice what the Lord said to those churches:

Repent and do the things you did at first. If you do not repent,
I will come to you and remove your lamp-stand from its place.
Revelation 2:5

Also 1 John 2:18-19. John mentions the presence of anti-christs in a local church — *and their removal.*

So, the Divine Gardener can remove sinning believers, and churches of sinning believers, from this scene of time.

I think we know what *'cutting off'* can mean.

4. What about *'cutting back'* to encourage *'fruit'*, *'more fruit' and 'much fruit'?* Are there biblical instances of this work of the Father?

Yes, there are!

The famous text in this connection is Hebrews 12:5-11 where the writer is quoting Proverbs 3:11-12.

Consider him who endured such opposition from sinful men, so that you will not grow weary and lose heart.
In your struggle against sin, you have not yet resisted to the point of shedding your blood.
And you have forgotten that word of encouragement that addresses you as sons:
> *"My son, do not make light of the Lord's discipline, and do not lose heart when he rebukes you, because the Lord disciplines those he loves, and he punishes everyone he accepts as a son."*
> Proverbs 3:11-12
Endure hardship as discipline; God is treating you as sons. For what son is not disciplined by his father? If you are not disciplined (and everyone undergoes discipline), then you are illegitimate children and not true sons.
Moreover, we have all had human fathers who disciplined us and we respected them for it. How much more should we submit to the Father of our spirits and live!
Our fathers disciplined us for a little while as they thought best; but God disciplines us for our good, that we may share in his holiness.

No discipline seems pleasant at the time, but painful. Later on, how-ever, it produces a harvest of righteousness and peace for those who have been trained by it. Heb. 12:3-11

We know now what <u>cutting back</u>, and <u>pruning</u> can mean.

We know that it is possible for believers to sin grievously and bring shame on the Name of Christ. Like so much of the New Testament, John 15 is on record to teach believers how to maintain a Christian testimony and glorify God.

If there are those who think they can waltz their way to heaven, having a good time by one means or another, living close to the world without becoming part of it *(as they imagine),* not taking the Christian life too seriously – they have another think coming to them.

Recall John 15:1-2

"I am the true vine, and my Father is the gardener. <u>He cuts off</u> every branch in me that bears no fruit, while every branch that does bear fruit <u>he prunes</u> so that it will be even more fruitful.

You may remember that we had got as far as v. 6
when we took time out to think deeply
about the teaching of Jesus.

Let us pause for a second time, before moving on, to ask about something that has been a considerable difficulty for many believers.

'WHAT IS THE FRUIT THAT THE BRANCHES OF THE VINE WILL BEAR? [vv. 2, 4-5, 8, 16]

Many preachers in the past thundered at their hearers that the fruit Jesus was talking about was *'new converts'* and if we were not seeing people come to faith in Christ as a direct result of our witness then we were not bearing fruit!

Consequently many sincere believers left meetings to make their way home overwhelmed by failure and despair.

WERE THOSE PREACHERS SPEAKING
TRUTH OR FALSEHOOD?

When Jesus spoke about the Holy Spirit
He said two things and said them clearly:

(1) *'He will testify* about Me.' 15:26

(2) He explained what the disciples will be doing:
   '*You also* must testify.' 15:27

Look ahead for a moment to 16:7-11.

Learn here that the Holy Spirit has a ministry to unbelievers that is uniquely His, and impossible for us:

He will convict the world of guilt in regard to sin and righteousness and judgment: in regard to sin because men do not believe in me, in regard to righteousness because I am going to the Father where you can see me no longer, and in regard to judgment, because the prince of this world now stands condemned. 16:7-11.

New believers are brought to faith in Christ through the unique ministry of the Holy Spirit.

The Holy Spirit may reveal Jesus to unbelievers directly or he may choose to speak to them through our witness.

Usually he does both.

The fruitfulness of believers is part and parcel of the way the Son glorifies the Father. (13:31)

Did you notice the things that Jesus emphasised in these chapters?

They are all aspects of Christian character i.e. the fruit of the Spirit.

The command to remain / live in Him. (15:7-8).

(This becomes tangible evidence that we are His disciples.)

The command to love Him: *by obeying His commands* (14:21, 23, 24)

The command to love one another: *'as I have loved you'* (15:12)

If these things are present in our lives then very soon 'the fruit of the Spirit' will appear in us. (Gal. 5:22-26)

Fruit-bearing for God is a human impossibility!

Fruit-bearing for God is the work of Christ in us.

DOES THAT ANSWER THE QUESTION?

If you and I will give due attention to our relationship with our Lord and Saviour, and place ourselves at His disposal to do with us as He wills, then in His time and way these branches will produce fruit for His glory and the glory of His Father.

If you remain in me and my words remain in you, ask whatever you wish, and it will be given you. 15:7
You did not choose me, but I chose you and appointed you to go and bear fruit—fruit that will last. Then the Father will give you whatever you ask in my name. John 15:16

The range of this promise is remarkable: v. 7 whatever you wish, and v. 16 whatever you ask

But read carefully because there is a condition attached.

'IF YOU *REMAIN / LIVE* IN ME
AND MY WORDS *REMAIN / LIVE* IN YOU (v. 7)

When we remain/live in Christ we are in harmony with God's purpose, the yearning of our hearts accords with his divine concerns, and so our praying is *'according to His will.'*

Prayer is crucial to the effective mission of believers in the world.

James reminds us that we *'have not, because we ask not.'*

Pay attention as Jesus continues where he left off in or about v 4-6

Jesus speaks about loving our fellow believers. vv. 7-9

In this section Jesus focuses on the command to love.

A Christ-like love between Christians
is a fundamental principle of Christian witness.

If you remain in me and my words remain in you, ask whatever you wish, and it will be given you.
This is to my Father's glory, that you bear much fruit,
showing your-selves to be my disciples.
"As the Father has loved me, so have I loved you. Now remain /
LIVE in my love. 15:7-9

Has the world ever seen such love?

Has the church ever seen such love?

What can we do to manifest this love?

Where shall we begin?

Jesus also speaks about obedience to him.
This is a fundamental principle of the Christian Life.

If you obey my commands, you will remain in my love, just as I have obeyed my Father's commands and remain in his love.

JESUS INTENDS THAT OUR RELATIONSHIP WITH HIM AND OUR SERVICE FOR HIM SHOULD BE FILLED WITH JOY.

I have told you this so that my joy may be in you and that your joy may be complete.

My command is this: Love each other as I have loved you.

Greater love has no-one than this that he lay down his life for his friends. 15:10-17

JESUS FINDS DELIGHT IN SHARING HIS PLANS WITH HIS PEOPLE BECAUSE THEY ARE HIS FRIENDS.

You are my friends if you do what I command.

I no longer call you servants, because a servant does not know his master's business. Instead, I have called you friends, for everything that I learned from my Father I have made known to you. vv. 14-17

OUR STANDING AND RELATIONSHIP WITH JESUS IS A MATTER OF GRACE FROM FIRST TO LAST.

You did not choose me, but I chose you and appointed you to go and bear fruit—fruit that will last.

Then the Father will give you whatever you ask in my name. This is my command: Love one another. v. 17

John 15 – Part Two

THE WORLD HATES THE DISCIPLES 15:18–16:4

Jesus speaks about the hostile world his people live in

"If the world hates you, keep in mind that it hated me first.
If you belonged to the world, it would love you as its own.
As it is, you do not belong to the world, but I have chosen you out
of the world.
That is why the world hates you. Remember the words I spoke to
you: 'No servant is greater than his master.'
If they persecuted me, they will persecute you also.
If they obeyed my teaching, they will obey yours also. 15:18-20

THE WORLD'S HATES US BECAUSE WE BELONG TO CHRIST

v. 18   The world hated Jesus before it hated us.

v. 19   If we belonged to the world, it would love us as its own.

v. 20   The world will treat us as it treated Him.

They will treat you this way because of my name, for they do not
know the One who sent me.
If I had not come and spoken to them, they would not be guilty
of sin.
Now, however, they have no excuse for their sin.
He who hates me hates my Father as well.
If I had not done among them what no-one else did, they would
not be guilty of sin.

But now they have seen these miracles, and yet they have hated both me and my Father.
But this is to fulfil what is written in their Law: 'They hated me without reason.' 15:21-25

THE WORLD HATES US BECAUSE IT DOESN'T KNOW THE FATHER

v. 21   The world rejects us because we are proclaiming a message.

vv. 22-24 The world's great sin is that it rejected the person and witness of Jesus.

v. 25   The Scriptures prophesied that the world would hate Jesus without a cause (Psalm 35:9 & 69:4).

FINALLY, JESUS GIVES HIS PEOPLE A TWO-FOLD PROMISE IN THESE CHAPTERS:

v. 26   When the Advocate comes, whom I will send to you from the Father – the spirit of truth who goes out from the Father – **he will testify about me.**

v. 27   **And you also must testify**, for you have been with me from the beginning.

Thank You, Heavenly Father:

For the heart to heart conversation that Jesus had with his disciples on the night on which he would be betrayed and for the privilege given us to share in it for our spiritual growth and well-being;

For the issues that were close to Jesus' heart then, and the relevance of all of them to our situation in today's world;

For the plainness and directness of what Jesus said about believers abiding/ remaining/ living in the Vine;

For the advent of the Holy Spirit, 'Christ's Other Self' who would come to abide with the disciples and with us until Jesus will come again;

For the precious words of Holy Scripture that never grow old, or irrelevant. They are always speaking if we will discipline ourselves to listen to them in today's noisy world.

In Jesus' Name, Amen.

Chapter 16

THE ADVENT OF THE HOLY SPIRIT

Part One
John 15:26–16:4

J ohn15: 26 & 27 are very important verses because they are connecting verses between the bulk of chapter 15 and all that lies ahead in the following chapters.

We thought about the important facts in these verses at the end of the previous study.

In v. 26 Jesus said of the Advocate: **He will testify about me.**

In v. 27 Jesus said of the disciples: **And you also will testify.**

This study begins at John 16:5 because the subject from the previous chapter over ran. I would have preferred chapter 15 to run on for another five verses. It is an unfortunate chapter division.

This is Jesus' final teaching opportunity before he is taken from them when he is arrested in the Garden of Gethsemane.

Jesus had been speaking about his departure, (v. 1, 4, 5, 7);

about the persecution the disciples will soon meet, (v. 20);

and about the coming of the Holy Spirit, (v. 7);

and about the conviction he will bring to the world. (vv. 8-11)

The chapter is bracketed by two facts about Jesus:

(1) He came from God; and (2) He is returning to God.

This is another very full chapter (like chapter 14) and so I will pick out the main and the supporting sections as we go along.

Part Two

JOHN 16:5-16
THE WORK OF THE HOLY SPIRIT

"Now I am going to him who sent me, yet none of you asks me, 'Where are you going?' Because I have said these things, you are filled with grief. 16:5-6

J esus would rather have his disciples asking him questions about his going away from them, than have them living under a cloud of grief. In their present mood they are focusing on themselves rather than on Him.

JESUS' DEPARTURE John 16:7

But I tell you the truth: It is for your good that I am going away. Unless I go away, the Counsellor will not come to you; but if I go, I will send him to you. 16:7

1. Jesus' departure is for the disciples' good.
2. When Jesus returns to the Father he will send the Counsellor / the Holy Spirit to them.
3. Jesus' departure will mark the completion of His work on their behalf.

After He has gone, the Holy Spirit will commence a special ministry of His own in the hostile world into which the disciples were sent by Jesus.

THE HOLY SPIRIT HAS A MINISTRY TO THE WORLD.

When he comes, he will convict the world of guilt in regard to sin and righteousness and judgment:

In regard to sin, because men do not believe in me;

In regard to righteousness, because I am going to the Father, where you can see me no longer;

And in regard to judgment, because the prince of this world now stands condemned. 16:8-11

THE WORLD is wrong about sin because it does not believe in Jesus. Their rejection of Jesus is their basic sin.

THE WORLD is wrong about righteousness because Jesus is going to the Father. The world sinned in condemning the righteous Son of God to death.

THE WORLD is wrong about judgment because the prince of this world now stands condemned. The world had condemned Jesus, but the Holy Spirit will reveal that it was the evil one who was judged and condemned by Jesus glorification.

THE DISCIPLES will bear witness to the great facts of Jesus' eternality, incarnation, life, baptism, temptation, ministry of teaching preaching and healing, his death, burial, resurrection, ascension and return in glory. This is the heart of gospel preaching. This is the groundwork.

THE HOLY SPIRIT will do a unique work in the hearts of unbelievers, an inward ministry to the consciences of sinners that
is utterly impossible for the disciples to perform.

*It is the Spirit's unique work, and not human preaching or per-
suasion that will do this work successfully, and bring sinners to
Jesus.* 16: 8-11

THE HOLY SPIRIT HAS A MINISTRY TO BELIEVERS.

*"I have much more to say to you, more than you can now bear.
But when he, the Spirit of truth, comes, <u>he will guide you
into all truth</u>.*

*He will not speak on his own; he will speak only what he hears,
and he will tell you what is yet to come.*

*He will bring glory to me by taking from what is mine and
making it known to you.*

All that belongs to the Father is mine.

*That is why I said the Spirit will take from what is mine and
make it known to you.*

*"In a little while you will see me no more, and then after a little
while you will see me."* 16:12-16

Notice how much information about the Holy Spirit is packed
into these verses.

In short, through the Spirit 'the disciples will share in the very
life of God that they have seen in Jesus. Their intimacy with
Jesus himself will be far deeper than before.'

The primary witness to Jesus in the world today is the
Christian community. They expose and condemn the world, in
particular by their love (13:35) and unity (17:21). Such love

and unity reveal that they are sharing in God's own life, and consequently, their rejection and persecution show that their opponents are acting against God. The very judgment that Jesus brought into the world continues through the disciples and elicits the same hatred.

THE HOLY SPIRIT HAS A MINISTRY TO JESUS

The Holy Spirit will focus on Jesus the Son and *will not speak on his own but will only speak what he hears* (v. 13).

Jesus had done exactly the same with respect to his Father (15:15). The Son has revealed the Father, and now the Spirit will reveal the Father by revealing the Son.

That was a profound answer Jesus gave to Philip in Ch. 14:9 *'Anyone who has seen me has seen the Father'*. Jesus' knowledge of his Father is complete and He has held nothing back from the disciples.

Jesus' staggering claim to have complete knowledge of God is the foundation for the Christian claim that Jesus is the unique and only way to the Father.

One more clarification before we move on: (v. 13*) 'He will not speak on his own; he will speak only what he hears, and he will tell you what is yet to come.*

This has been understood by many to mean that the Holy Spirit will give the disciples predictions of the future. Not so!

The expression *'what is yet to come'* is paralleled in the following verses with the phrase *'what is mine'* which suggests that the future events have to do with Jesus. At that point the future events included Jesus' glorification—the crucifixion, resurrection and ascension, his heavenly ministry and personal return in glory.

So Jesus' promise is not of new revelation, but of increasing insight into the one revelation found in Him.

Part Three

THE DISCIPLES' GRIEF WILL TURN TO JOY VV. 17-33

THE DISCIPLES ARE PUZZLED

"In a little while you will see me no more, and then after a little while you will see me."

<u>Jesus' comment in v. 16 prompted the discussion that follows.</u>

Some of his disciples said to one another, "What does he mean by saying, 'In a little while you will see me no more, and then after a little while you will see me,' and 'Because I am going to the Father'?"
They kept asking, "What does he mean by 'a little while'?
We don't understand what he is saying." 16:16-18

Things that are clear to us, because we have had a completed Bible all our lives through, may make the questions raised by the disciples seem rather childish. They did not have a clear grasp of what was coming next in their relationship with Jesus.

He gave them the opportunity to question him, rather than each other, to obtain a proper understanding of his remarks.

Jesus saw that they wanted to ask him about this, so he said to them, "Are you asking one another what I meant when I said, 'In a little while you will see me no more, and then after a little while you will see me'? 16:19

Jesus has two things to say in order to set them thinking.
I tell you the truth, you will weep and mourn while the world rejoices. You will grieve, but your grief will turn to joy. 16:20

He mentions two sets of circumstances, one marked by GRIEF and the other by JOY

<u>The disciples will grieve</u> – the weeping and mourning that Jesus refers to is the kind of public mourning that is seen when a local or national leader passes away. It can be a mere public display and can go on for a prolonged period of time

<u>The world will rejoice</u>. The Jesus the world hated has died and been buried.

<u>The disciples will grieve but their grief will turn to joy.</u> They will grieve at His suffering and death and burial. They will rejoice in a matter of days' time when Jesus appears to them after His resurrection.

<u>As an illustration of the joy they will experience</u> Jesus refers to a woman's pain in childbirth – and her utter joy when her child is born.

I tell you the truth, you will weep and mourn while the world rejoices. You will grieve, but your grief will turn to joy.
A woman giving birth to a child has pain because her time has come; but when her baby is born she forgets the anguish because of her joy that a child is born into the world.
So with you: Now is your time of grief, but I will see you again and you will rejoice, and no-one will take away your joy. 16:20-22

The resurrection of Jesus will never be undone! Therefore none can take the joy of it away from the Lord's people. No power in the entire universe can separate us from the love and presence of the Risen Jesus.

CHANGES ARE COMING IN THEIR RELATIONSHIP WITH THE FATHER AND WITH THE SON.

In that day you will no longer ask me anything. I tell you the truth, my Father will give you whatever you ask in my name.

Until now you have not asked for anything in my name. Ask and you will receive, and your joy will be complete.

"Though I have been speaking figuratively, a time is coming when I will no longer use this kind of language but will tell you plainly about my Father.

In that day you will ask in my name. I am not saying that I will ask the Father on your behalf.

No, the Father himself loves you because you have loved me and have believed that I came from God.

I came from the Father and entered the world; now I am leaving the world and going back to the Father." 16:23-28

Jesus reference to 'speaking figuratively' is a comment on the fact that there were things that He had to leave untold due to the incapacity of the disciples to receive them. A great change is coming. In the new era of the Holy Spirit all that God wants us to know will be clear, free, unrestricted and full. It will no longer be characterised by '*veiled utterances.'*

Jesus' references to' that day' is to Resurrection Day. It will mark the beginning of a new era: followed by His ascension and the outpouring of the Holy Spirit on the day of Pentecost.

From that day forward <u>He will be alive in the power of an end-less life.</u>

From that day forward <u>you will pray directly to the Father, in the authority of my Name.</u> That is the proper approach in all Christian prayer.

John Calvin comments*: 'We have the heart of God as soon as we place before him the name of his Son.'*

From that day forward <u>you will have the joy of answered prayer.</u>

Here is all that the disciples or ourselves can ever long for; enough for all and forever.

Part Four

CHRIST'S FAREWELL TO HIS DISCIPLES. V. 28

I came from the Father and entered the world;
now I am leaving the world and going back to the Father."

Two indisputable facts of world history and more importantly, salvation history stand like book-ends with the life of Christ between them – his incarnation and his resurrection ascension. **Then Jesus' disciples said,**

> *"Now you are speaking clearly and without figures of speech.*
> *Now we can see that you know all things and that you do not even*
> *need to have anyone ask you questions.*
> *This makes us believe that you came from God."*
> *"You believe at last!" Jesus answered. "But a time is coming, and*
> *has come, when you will be scattered, each to his own home. You*
> *will leave me all alone. Yet I am not alone, for* my *Father is with*
> *me.* 16:29-32

vv. 29-30 sound like a renewed profession of faith in Jesus on the part of the disciples. Jesus commends them (v. 31). Their enthusiasm is touching but not securely based.

> 'Like young recruits, they had yet to learn that it is one thing to
> know the soldier's drill and to wear the uniform, and quite another
> to be steadfast in battle.'

However Jesus knows what they do not know yet: their faith in Him will be tested and deepened enormously in the next few days. Everyone, without exception, will be scattered (v. 32).

They will all be scattered until they are gathered again beyond the cross by the Risen Lord, after *'a little while'*.

The Lord's time with them has almost gone. He speaks memorable words for their comfort.

"I have told you these things, so that in me you may have peace. In this world you will have trouble. But take heart! I have overcome the world." 16:33

JESUS HAS OVERCOME THE WORLD

(1) Because His Father was with Him. v. 32

(2) Because the last word lies, not with the evil one, but with the Father, and therefore with the Father's Everlasting Son and Servant.

Through His obedience unto death, death itself will fall defeated, and with it all the rebellious powers of darkness and sin.

When history closes the church will not be singing *'We have overcome . . .'* but rather *'Worthy is the Lamb, who was slain'*. Rev. 5:12.

Christ's Persecuted People are Home at Last!

Thank You, Heavenly Father:

For the teaching skills of Jesus Christ Your Son; our minds are stretched as we try to take in all that he shared with us in John chapter 16;

For the ongoing ministry of the Holy Spirit to us, to Jesus and
to the world in which we live; and for his ability to cut right
through the confusing schemes and temptations of the devil
as he blinds unbelievers to the truth of the gospel;

For the fact that if the Holy Spirit's threefold ministry were to
be withdrawn evangelism and gospel work would become
impossible; we thank you that we do not go alone to witness for Jesus – the SPIRIT witnesses and WE witness also.

In Jesus' Name. Amen.

Chapter 17

THE LORD'S PRAYER

Part One
Comments on 'the Lord's Prayer'

Since childhood I have known what is commonly called *'The Lord's Prayer.'* It is by no means a misnomer, for that is what it is. The title refers to the pattern prayer that Jesus gave His disciples in Matthew 5:9 (including the doxology with which it ends *'for thine is the kingdom, the power and the glory, forever and ever. Amen).*

When I was a small child I was taught to use it as part of my bedtime prayers.

When I first went to Sunday school I was taught it there, but I never remember us reciting it together as a whole Sunday school, or in the services of the Baptist Church to which the Sunday school was attached. I couldn't understand that.

When I went to Clooney Primary School in Londonderry I was taught it there, and sometimes the local Presbyterian minister, Rev. F. G. Bell, would conduct morning assembly for the whole school and we would say it together.

I've been a Minister of the Gospel for 50 years and I don't mind telling you that there were numerous times when I came up against a brick wall in my prayer life, and when I could find no other words, I prayed *'The Lord's Prayer'* that I had known as a child.

I doubt if anyone knows how much that prayer meant to the soldiers in Two World Wars and other conflicts; or how often it is used by people who make no Christian profession at all. If we only knew how much that prayer means when people have ended up in the gutter of life and memory brings it back to them. If we could know how much that simple prayer would mean to children at their present age and throughout their lives.

I will be the first to admit that using *'the Lord's Prayer'* (so-called) doesn't save anyone, but it is a prayer that even infant lips may try. It may be the only prayer that many people know.

Having made myself clear about what is popularly called **'The Lord's Prayer'** I want to hurry on and say that in John 17 there is a prayer that may properly be called **'THE LORD'S PRAYER.'** However, that is not its best known title.

Since the 5th Century AD this prayer has been referred to as

'THE HIGH PRIESTLY PRAYER'.

This title is much more appropriate because it marks the occasion when, prior to His passion and death on the cross, Jesus prayed this prayer for Himself, for His disciples and for those who would become believers through their witness.

Another title I discovered much more recently is
'JESUS' PRAYER OF CONSECRATION'
which I think is a very perceptive title.

If we ask **'Why did Jesus pray this prayer?** The answer lies in the opening verses of chapters 13 & 17.

> It was just before the Passover Feast. *Jesus knew that the time had come for him to leave this world and go to the Father.* Having loved his own who were in the world, he now showed them the full extent of his love. John 13:1
> After Jesus said this, he looked towards heaven and prayed: *"Father, the time has come. Glorify your Son, that your Son may glorify you.* 17:1

He knew that lots of important matters would have to be sandwiched between 13:1 and 17:1. Take a cursory glance at the NIV section headings and this becomes clear.

13:1-17	Jesus washes his disciples' feet.
13:18-30	Jesus predicts his betrayal
13:31-38	Jesus predicts peter's denial
14:1-14	Jesus comforts his disciples
14:15-31	Jesus promises the Holy Spirit
15:1-17	The Vine and the branches
15:18-16:4	The world hates the disciples
16:5-16	The work of the Holy Spirit
16:17-33	The disciples' grief will turn to joy

Now let us look ahead to what followed John 17: because these matters were also on Jesus' mind as he prayed.

18:1-11	Jesus arrested
18:12-14	Jesus taken to Annas
18:15-18	Peter's first denial
18:19-24	The high priest questions Jesus

18:25-27	Peter's second and third denials
18:28-40	Jesus before Pilate
19:1-16	Jesus sentenced to be crucified
19:17-27	The crucifixion of Jesus
19:28-37	The death of Jesus
19:38-42	The burial of Jesus

At this point all these events were hidden from the disciples, but Jesus was totally aware of them. His mind was running ahead in anticipation, and so He prayed.

IN THIS CONTEXT HIS PETITIONS IN JOHN 17:1-5 ARE VERY REVEALING.

We need to be very thoughtful as we approach this chapter. It takes us into the mind and heart of Jesus. There are few other Scriptures which do this at such length.

Is there anything more private in our relationship with God than our prayers? Was there anything more intimate in the life of Jesus than the words He used and the petitions He made when speaking to His Father in prayer?

Perhaps Jesus shared this prayer with his disciples after his resurrection when he moved freely from place to place in order to minister to them. We wonder who the privileged penman was.

Thank You, Heavenly Father:

For the great privilege of having on record the very prayer that Jesus prayed on the evening before his death: for himself, for his disciples, and for all believers; in this prayer we see into the mind and heart of our Saviour, whom we know loves to the uttermost;

For the fact that our Saviour's intercessions for us are being heard in heaven, even as we contemplate this remarkable, saving ministry of Jesus.

In Jesus' Name, Amen.

Chapter 17

THE LORD'S PRAYER

Part Two

JOHN 17 IS ONE OF THE GREATEST CHAPTERS OF THE BIBLE.

There is no prayer equal to this prayed by the Lord. There were other servants of God who were men of prayer and we hold them in high regard for their praying; but none can compare with Jesus in prayer.

We try to keep our curiosity in check, but we would like to know how John was able to record this prayer in full. This has not been revealed.

1. THERE MUST HAVE BEEN STRONG REASONS WHY JESUS PRAYED *AT THIS POINT.*

The Lord could not presume that the disciples had grasped the importance of everything he had said and done in chapters 13-16:

the foot washing,

the forthcoming betrayal by Judas and denials by Peter in ch.13;

the promise of a heavenly home and the advent of the Holy Spirit in Ch. 14;

the teaching about the Vine and the Branches in Ch. 15;
the work of the Holy Spirit in Ch. 16,
including the warning of the hostility the disciples
would meet with from the world.

There was no more time to talk about these things at any length.

The sum of what He had told them in the previous chapters is found in 16:28. *I came from the Father and entered the world; now I am leaving the world and going back to the Father."*

<u>Jesus knew that His disciples</u>
<u>were a very vulnerable group of men.</u>

2. BEFORE JESUS' FINAL CONFLICT IN HIS PASSION AND DEATH ON THE CROSS ONE MORE MINISTRY REMAINED TO BE PERFORMED: THE HOLY WORK OF PRAYER.

Jesus Himself felt the need of prayer. In a few minutes we shall examine His supplication (what He asked for himself.) Within 24 hours or so He would be giving Himself up to death in a new and specific act of obedience to His Father: therefore He prays.

Jesus prayed for His disciples, and also for those who would believe on Him through their witness. We shall examine these prayers in due course (what He asked for others). We shall find that He was well aware of their needs and brought them to His Father.

3. ANOTHER OBSERVATION ABOUT JESUS' PRAYER IS THAT REAL PRAYER HAS PURPOSE.

This is the very thing that so much of what we call *'prayer'* lacks! It is very easy to know when someone is *praying with purpose* and when they are merely talking *'off the top of their head'*

'Off the top of the head' prayers aren't very worshipful, nor are they edifying to those who have to listen to them. Do we expect them to be answered?

I wonder that congregations tolerate them. I wonder what Bible College Students are taught about prayer, particularly Pulpit Prayers.

A woman would not go shopping the way some folks pray. She doesn't shop as if she were a butterfly. She knows what she wants before she leaves home! She's shops more like a bee, bringing home the honey!

PURPOSE is written all over this prayer of Jesus.
It shows PRE-MEDITATION (forethought).

John 17:1-5

JESUS PRAYS FOR HIMSELF

1. JESUS' PRAYER FOR HIMSELF REVEALS AGREEMENT WITH HIS FATHER.

After Jesus said this, he looked towards heaven and prayed: "Father, the time has come. 17:1

Jesus used the name *'Father'* when He prayed. Twenty-one of His prayers are recorded in the Gospels and on every occasion He used the word 'Father' to address God (with the exception of *the cry of dereliction from the Cross*: Matthew 27:46).

There was a mutual understanding between Father and Son that the point that both were anticipating had arrived.

The *'hour'* for which Christ had come into the world had struck—the hour when the Son of God would offer Himself, the just for the unjust; the time when Satan's power would appear to engulf the Holy One.

Jesus did not ask for a lightening of the load He must bear, He did not ask for encouragement in any shape or form. He was not alarmed by the cross or the suffering it involved. He saw only a means of glorifying God His Father.

2. JESUS' PRAYER FOR HIMSELF REVEALS A SUPREME DESIRE TO HONOUR HIS FATHER.

Glorify your Son, that your Son may glorify you. 17:1

This was an utterly selfless prayer. He desired it for one reason:–that it would result in greater honour for His Father.

He has come afresh before His Father to deliberately present Himself in self-abandonment to His Father's purpose.

These moments of prayer are moments of supreme self-consecration. The Son of God seeks the Father's glory; the Father seeks the Son's.

This petition links chapter 13:31 and 17:1.

Jesus said, "Now is the Son of Man glorified and God is glorified in him. John 13:31
After Jesus said this, he looked towards heaven and prayed: "Father, the time has come. Glorify your Son, that your Son may glorify you. 17:1

3. JESUS' PRAYER FOR HIMSELF REVEALS ACCOUNTABILITY.

For you granted him authority over all people that he might give eternal life to all those you have given him. 17:2

This authority was given by the Father to Jesus only.

We ask: for what purpose? The answer is in v. 2:–*that he might give eternal life to all those you have given him.*

Was the purpose achieved? Read on to v. 4.

As Lord of all, Christ has authority to give life to all. Due to human unbelief not all will receive this life.

We ask: what is this life? And how is it received?

Now this is Eternal life: *that they may know you, the only true God.* 17:3

Eternal life is *not only everlasting life* – it is much, much more!

Eternal life is *knowing the Eternal God and Jesus Christ whom He has sent.*

I have brought you glory on earth *by completing the work you gave me to do.* 17:4

We stand in awe as we listen to The Son of God accounting to His Father for the authority that was given to Him.

To be sure, historically speaking, He had not yet suffered the cross, but He has a right to speak as if this suffering has already been endured, so certain it is that He will endure it!

4. JESUS' PRAYER FOR HIMSELF REVEALS A LONGING TO GO HOME TO HIS FATHER.

And now, Father, glorify me in your presence with the glory I had with you before the world began. John 17:5

The glory which Jesus had shared with His Father from before an orderly universe existed had never been absent from His mind.

To return again to the very presence of the Father so as to be face-to-face with Him is what He now requests.

Jesus is looking forward to the joy of his saved people, the very people whose salvation He (together with the Father and the Spirit) had planned from eternity, before the world existed.

Thank You, Heavenly Father:

For the fact that our Lord Jesus Christ has perfect knowledge of our circumstances and our needs;

For the lesson of the prayer–so far as we are concerned–is not for more of this world's goods, but for assurance that our real needs are always in our Lord's mind and his giving never ceases;

For the prophecy that Isaiah made (Isaiah 53) in which he spoke of Jesus, God's Suffering Servant, who would 'see of the travail of his soul and be satisfied;' our hearts long to bring him satisfaction every day we live.

For the learning experience it has been to discover that Jesus, who alone among men could say 'I do always those things that please Him,' still felt it incumbent upon him to *'give account of his work.'* John 17:2-3; 4-10; 12,

In Jesus' Name, Amen.

Chapter 17

THE LORD'S PRAYER

Part Three

JESUS PRAYS FOR HIS DISCIPLES

1. JESUS' PRAYER FOR HIS DISCIPLES REVEALS A SENSE OF OWNERSHIP

"I have revealed you to those whom you gave me out of the world. They were yours; you gave them to me and they have obeyed your word. 17:6

This emphasis continues in the following verses.

I pray for them. I am not praying for the world, but for those you have given me, for they are yours. 17:9

In v. 10 ownership is reciprocal and mutual:

All I have is yours, and all you have is mine. And glory has come to me through them. 17:10

How did the disciples become the property of the Father and the Son?

v. 7 speaks of them as KNOWING and v. 8 as BELIEVING.

Now they know that everything you have given me comes from you.

For I gave them the words you gave me and they accepted them.
They knew with certainty that I came from you, and they believed
that you sent me. 17:7-8

Recall the definition of eternal life in vv. 2-3

We may well ask:

what did they know?

Read the astonishing answer:

(1) that everything you have given me comes from you.

(2) they knew with certainty that I came from you

What did they believe?

(3)They believed that you sent me.

Trusting the words of Jesus brings its own authentication.

2. JESUS' PRAYER FOR HIS DISCIPLES REVEALS THEIR UTTER SECURITY.

Because they were *given to the Son by the Father* **these men were utterly secure.**

I am glad to tell you that this is true of every believer in Jesus Christ. You have been claimed by God, He has given you to His Son and you are utterly secure. On that basis how can anyone deny the doctrine of divine election?

It is a doctrine of assurance for all believers.

3. JESUS' PRAYER FOR HIS DISCIPLES REVEALS THAT HE RECEIVED GLORY FROM THEM.

All I have is yours, and all you have is mine.
And glory has come to me through them. 17:10

Not a word about their failings and immaturity! This is breath-taking! The very fact that God has saved deep-dyed sinners like us out of an ungodly society brings glory to Jesus Christ.

4. JESUS' PRAYER FOR HIS DISCIPLES REVEALS THEIR CHIEF NEEDS WHEN HE WILL HAVE RETURNED TO HEAVEN.

Jesus prayed for their protection (11, 12, 14, 15)

17:11-12

I will remain in the world no longer, but they are still in the world, and I am coming to you. Holy Father, protect them by the power of your name — **the name you gave me** — so that they may be one as we are one.

While I was with them, I protected them and kept them safe by that name you gave me. None has been lost except the one doomed to destruction so that Scripture would be fulfilled.

17:14

I have given them your word and the world has hated them, for they are not of the world any more than I am of the world.

17:15–16

My prayer is not that you take them out of the world but that you protect them from the evil one. They are not of the world, even as I am not of it.

They would encounter two formidable foes: *'the world which has hated them'* and *'the evil one'* (the devil). Jesus prayed that his disciples would have the protection of God's name.

5. JESUS PRAYED FOR THEIR UNITY (11 & 21)

V 11: Unity when under spiritual assault from the world

V. 21: Unity in their witness to the world.

THE EXCEPTION OF JUDAS
John 17:12

While I was with them, I protected them and kept them safe

by that name you gave me.

None has been lost except the one doomed to

destruction so that Scripture would be fulfilled.

Jesus is referring to the defection of Judas. It is difficult for us to get our heads round the condition and the ultimate position of this man. Notice the words Jesus used of him: *'the one doomed to destruction.'*

Recall also what Luke wrote about him in Acts 1:25

'Show us which of these two you have chosen

to take over this apostolic ministry,

which Judas left to go where he belongs.'

Judas willingly and wilfully sold His Lord for thirty pieces of silver. He was responsible for his actions. In perpetrating his foul deed.Judas knew he was doing wrong: his conscience told him so. This explains his suicide. Unconsciously Judas was fulfilling Scripture: **Psalm 41:9 & Zechariah 11:12**

6. JESUS PRAYED FOR THEIR JOY

"I am coming to you now, but I say these things while I am still in the world, so that they may have the full measure of my joy within them. 17:13

Jesus never wanted the service of His disciples to become drudgery!

He had joy in serving His Father, both before and following his death (Heb 12:1-2). He prayed that they also would be joyful people who serve joyfully.

Neither hostility from without nor the apostasy from within quenched the joy of Jesus, nor need it do so in the case of the disciples.

How many of us find joy in serving Jesus?

7. JESUS PRAYED FOR THEIR SANCTIFICATION

Sanctify them by the truth; your word is truth. As you sent me into the world, I have sent them into the world. For them I sanctify myself, that they too may be truly sanctified. 17:16-19

The word *'sanctify'* means to set apart for a specific purpose. In religious or liturgical usage it means *'set apart for a holy purpose."*

Jesus' life modelled sanctification. He never deviated from the service of His heavenly Father. In doing so He also served his fellowmen. Multitudes of people were blessed through the life and ministry of Jesus *'who went about doing good.'*

It was Jesus' devotion to his Father that best fitted Him for the work that was given Him to do.

As a disciple of Jesus 'lives in the Word (the Scriptures)' he or she will be best fitted to serve the Lord and be a blessing to their fellows.

Sanctification does not mean *'living in a ghetto'* – it means that *'we have been sent into the world.' (v. 18)*

'Being sent' meant for Jesus his utter dedication to the claim and call of His Father. The disciples' commission can mean nothing less, thus Jesus' prayer is *'sanctify them by the truth.'*

Thank You, Heavenly Father:

For the insights there are in the prayer of Jesus in John 17; we are only beginning to understand what our real and constant needs are, while we are in this hostile world;

For the fact that his ministry for us (prior to his death on the cross) was utterly essential to our well-being in today's world; Make us wise as we serve our Saviour here; Make us effective witnesses for Jesus;

In Jesus' Name, Amen.

Chapter 17

THE LORD'S PRAYER

Part Four

John 17:20-26

JESUS PRAYS FOR ALL BELIEVERS

1. THAT JESUS PRAYED FOR ALL BELIEVERS MEANS THAT HE PRAYED FOR US.

This section of the prayer is very moving because it brings Jesus into direct relationship with us.

There are two major petitions: vv. 20-23 & vv. 24-26

THE FIRST MAJOR PETITION vv. 20-23
'That the church may be united'

"My prayer is not for them alone. I pray also for those who will believe in me through their message, that all of them may be one, Father, just as you are in me and I am in you.
May they also be in us so that the world may believe that you have sent me.
I have given them the glory that you gave me, that they may be one as we are one: I in them and you in me.
May they be brought to complete unity to let the world know that you sent me and have loved them even as you have loved me.
17:20-23

W e are among those who believed in Him through the faithful ministry of the apostles and others down the centuries.

HIS PRAYER FOR US IS

(v. 20) that all of them may be one;

(v. 22) that they may be one as We are;

(v. 23) may they be brought to complete unity.

FOR WHAT PURPOSE?

(v. 20), *that all of them may be one, Father, just as you are in me and I am in you;*

(v. 21) May they also be in us so that the world may believe that you have sent me;

(v. 23) May they be brought to complete unity to let the world know that you sent me and have loved them even as you have loved me.

THIS UNITY is not brought about by human ingenuity,

(v. 22) *but by Jesus giving us the glory that the Father had given Him.'*

THIS UNITY is supernatural.

It is defined and included in the unity of the Father and the Son (v. 22 *as we are one*).

When Paul exhorted the Christians in Ephesus to *'keep the unity of the Spirit'* they were not to create it, but to maintain it and express it.'

THIS UNITY is tangible.

(v. 22) It will cause the world to believe that Jesus was sent by the Father and (v. 23) that the Father loves the church!

THIS UNITY is evangelical.

(v. 20) *I pray also for those who will believe in me through their message,* (vv. 21 & 23) *that the world may believe that you have sent me.*

The mission of the Church is nothing other than the continuation of the mission of its Lord.

THE QUESTION IS:
WHAT ARE WE GOING TO DO ABOUT IT?

THE SECOND MAJOR PETITION vv. 24-26
'That Jesus' mission may be completed'

"Father, I want those you have given me to be with me where I am, and to see my glory, the glory you have given me because you loved me before the creation of the world.
"Righteous Father, though the world does not know you, I know you, and they know that you have sent me.
I have made you known to them, and will continue to make you known in order that the love you have for me may be in them and that I myself may be in them." 17:24-26

Here is the finishing of the work the Father gave Him to do, the presentation of all those whom the Father has given Him, from all the ages and from around the globe, before Him who sits on the throne (Rev. 5:13).

We have seen the glory of Jesus
(the glory given Him by His Father) in the Scriptures.
We shall one day be with Jesus where He is!

In the meantime let us pray for a great inflowing of the love of the Father and the Son into our cold hearts.

Let us also pray for a great outflowing of that love to all who are our brothers and sisters in Christ in every land so that a watching world may believe in Jesus.

Thank You, Heavenly Father;

For revealing to us the difference between the prayers of Jesus and our own praying;

For the way Jesus' praying shed a flood of light on his relationship with You, his heavenly Father;

For how his praying for his disciples revealed so much about his relationship with them;

For how his prayers for us, who would become believers down the centuries are still being answered;

For the comfort it brings us to know that we have a praying Saviour who makes intercession for us with groanings that cannot be uttered.

In Jesus' Name, Amen.

Chapter 18

I t is said that more people are converted to faith in Jesus Christ through reading the Gospel of John than any other part of the Scriptures. I don't know how that statement could be proved, but it may be true.

Most people will agree that John's Gospel is different to the others in that it bears the marks of a mature writer and believer. John the beloved disciple would fulfil that qualification. He wrote his Gospel later in the 1st century therefore it is more theological than the others.

I am sure that we all have our own reasons for valuing this Gospel.

Chapters 1 -12   **Jesus' Local Ministry**

Chapters 13 – 12   **Jesus' Private Ministry**

Chapters 18 -21   **Jesus' Passion, Death and Resurrection.**

Please note some 'historical markers'.

John 13:1

It was just before the Passover Feast.

This means that it was THURSDAY

(Maundy Thursday) of Passion Week.

Please notice also the second half of the verse.

Jesus knew that the time had come for him to leave this world and go to the Father.

This reference is to the programme within which Jesus lived in harmony with the will of His heavenly Father.

John 18:1

When he had finished praying,

Jesus left with his disciples and crossed the Kidron Valley.

Other gospels identify the place as the Garden of Gethsemane.

In the context of all the gospels we know it is now **THURSDAY EVENING**, either the closing hours of the day or the small hours of FRIDAY MORNING).

John 18:28

Then the Jews led Jesus from Caiaphas to the palace of the Roman governor. <u>By now it was early morning,</u> (early FRIDAY MORNING) and to avoid ceremonial uncleanness the Jews did not enter the palace; they wanted to be able to eat the Passover.

Please bear in mind that Jesus had neither rest nor sleep since Wednesday night! His captors have kept him awake through Thursday night into Friday morning. We are about to discover the stress and strain and suffering that Jesus underwent at the hands of his captors. Hence the title of this study: -

John 18:1–11

JESUS ARRESTED

We notice a number of things about Jesus in the hands of his captors.

By comparison with Jesus the behaviour of Judas was that of a knave–utterly despicable. vv. 2-3

Judas used insider information about Jesus' prayer-habits when he led the detachment of soldiers to arrest Jesus in the Garden of Gethsemane. v. 2

> *Now Judas, who betrayed him, knew the place, because Jesus had often met there with his disciples.* 18:2

The detachment of soldiers who came with Judas was out of all proportion to the non-threatening person they had come to arrest. v. 3

> *So Judas came to the grove, guiding a detachment of soldiers and some officials from the chief priests and Pharisees. They were carrying torches, lanterns and weapons.* 18:3

By comparison with Judas the behaviour of Jesus was that of a King–utterly dignified. vv. 4-7

> *Jesus, knowing all that was going to happen to him, went out and asked them, "Who is it you want?"*
> *"Jesus of Nazareth," they replied. v. 4*

*"I am he," Jesus said. (And Judas the traitor was standing there
with them.)*
*When Jesus said, "I am he," they drew back and fell to the ground.
Again he asked them, "Who is it you want?" And they said, "Jesus
of Nazareth." 18:4-9*

Jesus had a complete knowledge of what was going to
happen to him. This sentence summarises the whole event,
indeed the whole of the Passion story. v. 4

He voluntarily made himself available to those who had
come to arrest him. v. 4

When he identified himself to the soldiers and those who
were with them he used the Divine Name: 'I AM'. v. 4

At the mention of that Name–*they drew back and fell to the
ground. v. 4*

Whether something of Jesus' divine majesty broke in upon
them for a moment–or they experienced a sudden wave of terror
as they were faced with laying hands on one whose supernatural
powers were already legend, we are not told.

Either way there is a perceptible loss of control on the part
of the authorities.

Jesus relieved the situation by re-identifying himself. vv. 7-8

With a pastoral heart Jesus then requested safe passage for
his disciples.

[8]"I told you that I am he," Jesus answered.
"If you are looking for me, then let these men go."
[9]This happened so that the words he had spoken would be fulfilled:
"I have not lost one of those you gave me." 18:8-9

Some words Jesus had spoken to the disciples (recorded in 6:39) are noted by John as having been fulfilled at that moment. This statement of Jesus is quoted in the same way as the Old Testament quotations studded through the gospel. v. 9

What shall we say about the behaviour of Jesus when Judas betrayed Him?

When those to whom Judas had betrayed Jesus came to arrest Him He requested safe passage for the disciples and voluntarily surrendered himself to be led away.

Then Simon Peter, who had a sword, drew it and struck the high priest's servant, cutting off his right ear. (The servant's name was Malchus.) Jesus commanded Peter, "Put your sword away! 18:10-11

Peter's action was unpremeditated and reckless. By comparison with the violence of Peter Jesus' submission to what He knew was the Father's will for him was awesome.

Shall I not drink the cup the Father has given me?"

The burden of Jesus' praying in the darkness of Gethsemane was uppermost in His mind amid all the pressures around Him.

The battle for our salvation had been fought and won when Jesus had submitted to His Father's will. He will not now or ever take up arms in the cause of His kingdom. The cup of God's judgment, the symbol of His righteous wrath is already in hands of God's beloved Son.

What shall we say about the behaviour of Jesus when Peter used violence to defend Him?

When Peter resorted to violence to defend Jesus
He put a stop to it because He had already
accepted *'the cup'* the Father had given Him.

John 18: 12–14

JESUS TAKEN TO ANNAS

Then the detachment of soldiers with its commander and the Jewish officials arrested Jesus. They bound him and brought him first to Annas, who was the father-in-law of Caiaphas, the high priest that year. Caiaphas was the one who had advised the Jews that it would be good if one man died for the people. 18:12-14

There was a lot of cronyism in the appointment of the High Priest. It was to be an annual appointment. However, when both the Jews and the Romans appointed their own nominees to the office there was confusion in the sanctuary (as in the days of John the Baptist).

Annas had been in office from AD 6 to 15; in the years since then no less than four of his sons held the office – and Caiaphas was his son-in-law. In every sense Annas was the power behind the throne and so claims *'first go'* at Jesus. In John's reporting the proceedings before Annas are interrupted by events in the courtyard outside.

John 18: 15–18

PETER'S FIRST DENIAL

Simon Peter and another disciple were following Jesus. Because this disciple was known to the high priest, he went with Jesus into the high priest's courtyard, but Peter had to wait outside at the door.

The other disciple, who was known to the high priest, came back, spoke to the girl on duty there and brought Peter in.

"You are not one of his disciples, are you?" the girl at the door asked Peter. He replied, "I am not."

It was cold, and the servants and officials stood round a fire they had made to keep warm. Peter also was standing with them, warming himself. 18:15-18

Peter gained access to the high priest's courtyard because he was vouched for by the other (unknown) disciple who was with him. vv. 15-16.

No sooner were they through the door than the girl who was the gate-keeper recognised Peter:

"You are not one of his disciples, are you?" the girl at the door asked Peter. He replied, "I am not."

Peter, caught completely off guard, answers to the contrary and denies His association with Jesus.

It was cold, and the servants and officials stood round a fire they had made to keep warm. Peter also was standing with them, warming himself.

It was a very miserable Peter who warmed himself at the fire.

John 18: 19–24

ANNAS QUESTIONS JESUS

Meanwhile, the high priest questioned Jesus about his disciples and his teaching. 18:19

These are the two areas on which the High Priest attempts to incriminate Jesus.

"I have spoken openly to the world," Jesus replied.
"I always taught in synagogues or at the temple, where all the Jews come together.
I said nothing in secret.
Why question me?
Ask those who heard me. Surely they know what I said."_John 18:20-21

I don't see the prisoner trembling. His voice is strong and calm. He can look the High Priest straight in the eye. If there is any heresy alleged, then let the witnesses produced and interrogated.

Jesus is protesting that no witnesses have been called. He is actually calling for a just trial. The essence of the Jewish legal process was the sworn testimony of witnesses. If two witnesses agreed in essentials, then the accused was doomed, no matter what he might say in his defence.

At this stage one of the officials took it upon himself to slap Jesus across the face, a painful foretaste of what was still to come.

When Jesus said this, one of the officials nearby struck him in the face. *"Is this the way you answer the high priest?"* he demanded. John 18:22

But Jesus is unbowed.

"If I said something wrong," Jesus replied, *"testify as to what is wrong. But if I spoke the truth, why did you strike me?"* 18:23-24

What shall we say about the behaviour of Jesus in the house of Annas?

The attempt of Annas the High Priest to draw Jesus into an incriminating admission about His disciples and His teaching failed because of the complete integrity of the prisoner.

Then Annas sent him, still bound, to Caiaphas the high priest.

Annas, outmanoeuvred by Jesus' complete integrity, can get no further and sends him on to his son-in-law Caiaphas.

PETER'S SECOND AND THIRD DENIALS

T he scene moves outside again. Meanwhile Jesus is being taken to the Palace of Pilate the Roman Governor.

As Simon Peter stood warming himself, he was asked, *"You are not one of his disciples, are you?"* He denied it, saying, *"I am not."* 18:25

Peter is still at the fire, and' under fire'! Having lied once, it is easy to lie a second time. He denies any association with Jesus.

*One of the high priest's servants, a relative of the man whose ear Peter had cut off, challenged him, **"Didn't I see you with him in the olive grove?"** 18:26*

'Peter! Be Careful! This accuser has irrefutable evidence!'

Again Peter denied it, and at that moment a cock began to crow. 18:27

Words were unnecessary – the cock crowing convicted Peter to the depths of his soul of the horror of what he had done with Jesus.

Jesus' foreknowledge was vindicated (13:38)
Then Jesus answered,

"Will you really lay down your life for me?
I tell you the truth, before the cock crows,
you will disown me three times!

As Jesus testified faithfully, Peter denied Him pathetically.

With the cock-crow Peter's wretched apostasy is suddenly exposed to him, and 'he went outside and wept bitterly.

What shall we say about Jesus' behaviour when
He knows that Peter is denying Him?

Peter cowered before his questioners in the High Priest's courtyard, denying everything;

Jesus stood up to his questioners in the Court of Caiaphas denying nothing.

John 18: 28–40

JESUS BEFORE PILATE

Then the Jews led Jesus from Caiaphas to the palace of the Roman
governor. By now it was early morning (i.e. FRIDAY MORNING)
and to avoid ceremonial uncleanness the Jews did not enter the
palace; they wanted to be able to eat the Passover. 18:28

These men, whom we may conveniently label 'OFFICIAL ISRAEL' were a bundle of contradictions. They have scruples of conscience regarding uncleanness for the Passover but have none at all about putting an innocent prisoner to death.

Pilate is co-operating nicely. He has honoured their scruples by actually coming out of his palace to speak with them.

> *So Pilate came out to them and asked,*
> *"What charges are you bringing against this man?"* 18:29

To which he received a short reply.

> *"If he were not a criminal,"* they replied,
> *"we would not have handed him over to you."* 18:30

But Pilate wasn't in a mood to be bothered.

> Pilate said, *"Take him yourselves and judge him by your own law."*
> *"But we have no right to execute anyone,"*
> the Jews objected. 18:31

Listen to their malevolence! They had brought him to Pilate with a view to securing Jesus' execution.

John opens a little window for his readers at this point.

This happened so that the words Jesus had spoken indicating the kind of death he was going to die would be fulfilled.

The Jews don't know it – but Jesus had already spoken of how he would be put to death

But I, when I am lifted up from the earth, will draw all men to myself." He said this to show the kind of death he was going to die. **18:32**

Pilate then went back inside the palace, summoned Jesus and asked him, *"Are you the king of the Jews?"*

"Is that your own idea," **Jesus asked,** *"or did others talk to you about me?"*
"Am I a Jew?" **Pilate replied.** *"It was your people and your chief priests who handed you over to me. What is it you have done?"* **18:33-35**

Pilate was at a loss to know what wrong-doing Jesus had been charged with. He hadn't been *'instructed'* – as our legal profession would say.

Jesus said, *"My kingdom is not of this world. If it were, my ser-*vants **would fight to prevent my arrest by the Jews. But now my kingdom is from another place." 18:36**

Jesus is not intimidated in the presence of this Roman Official.

"You are a king, then!" said **Pilate.**

Jesus answered, *"You are right in saying I am a king. In fact, for this reason I was born, and for this I came into the world, to testify to the truth. Everyone on the side of truth listens to me."*
Pilate is both relieved and provoked! *"You are a king, then!"*
This is the first word of testimony from the prisoner himself.
18:37 *"What is truth?" Pilate asked.*
With this he went out again to the Jews and said, "I find no basis for a charge against him. 18:38

Pilate asked Jesus: 'What is truth? but he didn't wait for an answer. Nor did he declare himself on the side of truth Pilate's judicial finding could have ended it all, and it should have done so. Perversely, Pilate could not leave it there.

He remembers that there is another card to play that will enhance his standing in the eyes of the Jews.

> *But it is your custom for me to release to you one prisoner at the time of the Passover.*
> *Do you want me to release 'the king of the Jews'?"*
> *They shouted back, "No, not him! Give us Barabbas!"*

Now Barabbas had taken part in a rebellion. 18:39-40
Please turn to 1 Timothy 6:13 where Paul refers to
Jesus' trial before Pilate.

> *In the sight of God, who gives life to everything, and of <u>Christ Jesus,</u> <u>who while testifying before Pontius Pilate made the good confes-</u> <u>sion,</u> I charge you to keep this command without spot or blame until the appearing of our Lord Jesus Christ,* 1 Timothy 6:13-14

What then shall we say about
the behaviour of Jesus before Pilate?

When Jesus stood before Pilate He witnessed a good confession: (18:37-38) He openly declared Himself to be a King, and invited Pilate to stand on the side of truth.

More than any other human being
Pontius Pilate had most to do with the death of Jesus Christ.
In 19:5 Pilate says of Jesus:
'Behold the man! / 'Here is the man!'
The choice that faced the mob in Jerusalem
is still before our world.
Who is our King? Jesus or Barabbas?

The world still chooses. So must we all

Thank You, Heavenly Father:

For the calmness of Jesus when he was arrested in the Garden of Gethsemane;

For his forbearance when he was arrested and then arraigned before the high priest and treated with extreme cruelty from the soldiers;

For the tremendous help that Jesus received from heaven when undergoing trial and torture;

For the testimony of Peter when writing his first letter to Christians scattered around the Roman Empire: *Christ suffered for you, leaving you an example, that you should follow his steps. 'He committed no sin, and no deceit was found in his mouth'. When they hurled their insults at him he did not retaliate; when he suffered, he made no threats. Instead, he entrusted himself to him who judges righteously.* 1 Peter 2:21-23

In Jesus' Name, Amen.

Chapter 19

LORD OF THE CROSS OF SHAME

When reading the Bible we need to remember that chapter and verse divisions were not in the original manuscripts.

Archbishop Stephen Langton and Cardinal Hugo de Sancto Caro developed different schemas for systematic division of the Bible in the early 13th century (i.e. 1200s).

It is the system of Archbishop Langton on which the modern chapter divisions are based (he was Archbishop of Canterbury from 1207 until his death in 1228).

The first Bible in English to use both chapters and verses was the Geneva Bible published in 1560.

We should be grateful that chapter and verse divisions are in modern Bibles, otherwise it would take us a long time to find the place for Scripture Reading in public worship, or even in personal reading.

Usually chapter divisions occur more or less in the right places. Occasionally we may wish they had occurred a sentence or paragraph earlier or later, as the case may be.

When we left chapter 18 Jesus was before Pilate. But there was more of that encounter still to be told. It will take until verse 16 of chapter 19 before the section ends.

So I would have preferred John 18 to continue to John 19:16.

Now we are moving into chapter 19. The title is:

JESUS: LORD OF THE CROSS OF SHAME VV. 1-16

It was Canon Michael Saward of St Paul's Cathedral in London who gave us this lovely name for Jesus. We shall use each of the three verses as the theme of the final three chapters of this gospel.

Lord of the cross of shame,
set my cold heart aflame
with love for you, my Saviour and my Master;
who on that lonely day
bore all my sins away,
and saved me from the judgement and disaster.

I am grateful to The Jubilate Group, Chelston, Torquay, Devon for permission to use this hymn by Canon Michael Saward. I think it will become apparent why I chose to use it in this book. It is a hymn that is truly devotional.

As we go through these 16 verses please note

THE SHAME JESUS ENDURED ON HIS WAY TO THE CROSS.

The encounter with Jesus had raised some personal issues for Pilate. Pilate found himself in the presence of a KING, such a king as he had never met before; whose kingdom was not of this world; who invited him to cross over to the side of truth (18:37).

Pilate was less than serious or sincere when speaking to Jesus.

He asked Jesus the question: *'What is truth'* (18:38) but didn't wait to hear the answer.

The guilt or innocence of Jesus was beside the point when Pilate offered the Jews the choice of having Jesus or Barabbas released to them.

He thought he could achieve Jesus' release by offering him as the Passover amnesty prisoner.

The crowd shouted back,

'No, not him! Give us Barabbas!' (18:39-40)

Then Pilate took Jesus and had him flogged. 19:1

This was shameful treatment. Pilate could have stopped it. He didn't have to give the order in the first place. The prisoner was shown no respect whatsoever.

The Romans had three levels of flogging:

Was this the *fustigatio?* a lighter beating for lesser offences?

Was this the *flogellatio?* a brutal flogging for more serious crimes?

Or was this the *verberatio?* the most terrible of all, which was administered as part of the preliminary to crucifixion?

It is not surprising to hear that prisoners not infrequently collapsed and died under this procedure

Physical beating was followed by further cruelty.

The soldiers twisted together a crown of thorns and put it on his head. They clothed him in a purple robe and went up to him again and again, saying, "Hail, king of the Jews!" And they struck him in the face. 19:2-3

So Jesus becomes the plaything of the Roman soldiers.

Their mood is – *'He's a King! We'll treat him like a king! A king needs a crown! – thorns will do nicely!'* Great jagged spikes from the date palm – up to 12 inches in length at times. They mesh them together and ram the mock crown on Jesus' head. *'A king needs a robe!'* So they found an old purple sheet and threw it round him.

Matthew and Mark say *they found a staff and pushed it into his hands as a sceptre.* 'Let the coronation proceed! Let the sport begin!

So they come forward in mocking homage *'Hail! King of the Jews! – and then the spit, the slap and the punch in the face.*

When they have taken their fill of violence they send Jesus back to Pilate and the crowd.

Once more Pilate came out and said to the Jews, *"Look, I am bringing him out to you to let you know that I find no basis for a charge against him."* 19:4

When Jesus came out wearing the crown of thorns and the purple robe, Pilate said to them, *"Here is the man!"* John 19:5

Pilate's verdict doesn't please the crowd.

As soon as the chief priests and their officials saw him, they shouted, *"Crucify! Crucify!"* But Pilate answered, *"You take *him and crucify him. As for me, I find no basis for a charge against him."* 19:6

The crowd is implacable.

The Jews insisted,

"We have a law, and according to that law he must die, because he claimed to be the Son of God." 19:7

Here the real basis of their accusation is laid bare. They had brought Him before Pilate on a religious charge. Religion makes Pilate uncomfortable.

When Pilate heard this, he was even more afraid, and he went back inside the palace. *"Where do you come from?"* he asked Jesus, but Jesus gave him no answer. 19:8-9

Pilate is alarmed at Jesus' divine claims – and probably affected by a message *his* wife had sent him *'Have nothing to do with this innocent man'* because she had had a nightmare about him.

Pilate doesn't know if Jesus is from earth or heaven. Is this some *'other-worldly visitor'* he has on his hands? Jesus doesn't make it easy for Pilate – He refuses to reply.

Pilate is exasperated and annoyed.

"Do you refuse to speak to me?" Pilate said.
"Don't you realise I have power either to free you or to crucify you?" 19:10

Pilate is relying on the authority of Tiberias Caesar in Rome. Jesus is conscious of an authority infinitely greater than any wielded by Pilate, or Caiaphas, or the Jewish mob, an authority in whose hands these human forces are but reeds in the wind.

Jesus answered,

"You would have no power over me if it were not given to you from above. Therefore the one who handed me over to you is guilty of a greater sin." 19:11

These are remarkable words from a man whose body is suffering the most excruciating agony from the brutality he had suffered from flogging and abuse.

From then on, Pilate tried to set Jesus free, but the Jews kept shouting,

"If you let this man go, you are no friend of Caesar. Anyone who claims to be a king opposes Caesar." 19:12

Roman sources record that Pilate had been honoured as 'a friend of Caesar' some time previously. The Jews' taunts were a strike at Pilate's pride and prestige. When Pilate heard this, he brought Jesus out and sat down on the judge's seat at a place known as the Stone Pavement (which in Aramaic is Gabbatha).

It was the day of Preparation of Passover Week, about the sixth hour. *"Here is your king,"* Pilate said to the Jews. 19:13-14

But they shouted,

"Take him awa but Caesar," the chief priests answered. 19:15

That sentence spoken by the Jews revealed the true state of Judaism.

In those few words 'OFFICIAL ISRAEL' had renounced their sacred covenant with God! They had denied God's kingship! They had abandoned the Messianic hope of Israel!

Finally Pilate handed him over to them to be crucified.

So the soldiers took charge of Jesus. 19:16

PILATE has lost.

THE TRIAL is over.

JESUS will die.

THE CRUCIFIXION
JOHN 19:17-27

As we go through these verses think about
THE SUFFERING JESUS EXPERIENCED WHEN
NAILED TO THE CROSS

Carrying his own cross, he went out to the place of the Skull (which in Aramaic is called Golgotha).
Here they crucified him, *and with him two others—one on each side and Jesus in the middle.* 19:17-18

Try to imagine the scene and what Jesus suffered there.

He was *a real man*—with a body that was completely human, that bled when wounded and hurt when abused.

His suffering was *physical. His body bore many wounds. His hands and feet were nailed to the cross, His side was pierced with a soldier's spear.*

His suffering was *at the hands of others.* He knows what it is to be abused. He is the God of the abused.

His suffering was *emotional. He felt incalculable shame. He looked a mess. He was exposed to ridicule. He was despised and we esteemed him not (Isaiah 53:3)*

His suffering was *substitutionary.* Centuries before the prophet Jeremiah has said *'Is it nothing to you, all you who pass by? Look around and see. Is there any suffering like my suffering that was inflicted on me that the Lord brought on me in the day of his fierce anger?'* Lamentations 1:12

Pilate had a notice prepared and fastened to the cross.

It read:

JESUS OF NAZARETH, THE KING OF THE JEWS.

Many of the Jews read this sign, for the place where Jesus was crucified was near the city, and the sign was written in Aramaic, Latin and Greek. 19:19-20

The title Pilate had prepared for attaching to the cross was written in the three major languages of the day:

LATIN   the language of Government

ARAMAIC   the language of the people (local Heb. dialect)

GREEK   the language of culture and learning.

The title incensed the Jewish leaders.

The chief priests of the Jews protested to Pilate, *"Do not write 'The King of the Jews', but that this man claimed to be king of the Jews."*

Pilate answered, *"What I have written, I have written."* 19:21-22

John adds two further notes.

What happened to Jesus' garments (his personal effects)?

When the soldiers crucified Jesus, they took his clothes, dividing them into four shares, one for each of them, with the undergarment remaining. This garment was seamless, woven in one piece from top to bottom.
"Let's not tear it," they said to one another.
"Let's decide by lot who will get it."
This happened that the scripture might be fulfilled which said,

"They divided my garments among them and cast lots for my cloth-ing."(Psalm 22:18)
So this is what the soldiers did. 19:23-24

John notes the presence of loyal friends and supporters.

Near the cross of Jesus stood his mother, his mother's sister, Mary the wife of Clopas, and Mary Magdalene.
When Jesus saw his mother there, and the disciple whom he loved standing near by, he said to his mother,
"Dear woman, here is your son," and to the disciple, "Here is your mother." From that time on, this disciple took her into his home.
19:25-27

Jesus committed his mother Mary to the care of John, the beloved disciple. Why not to one of his brothers? At that point they were unbelievers. In the care of John she would have a believing and supportive relationship.

John 19:28-37

THE DEATH OF JESUS

As we go through these verses let us meditate on
THE SACRIFICE JESUS MADE
WHEN HE DIED ON THE CROSS

Later, knowing that all was now completed, and so that the Scripture would be fulfilled, Jesus said, "I am thirsty." (Psalm 69:3 & 21) A jar of wine vinegar was there, so they soaked a sponge in it, put the sponge on a stalk of the hyssop plant, and lifted it to Jesus' lips When he had received the drink, Jesus said, "It is finished." With that, he bowed his head and gave up his spirit. 19:28-30

Please note the words in v. 28
knowing that all was now completed
and so that the Scripture would be fulfilled,

Jesus' mind was full of scripture throughout His life, from boyhood to manhood – it was His meat and drink. Here on the cross His mind is *'stayed upon Jehovah.'*

Jesus said, "It is finished."

Jesus died at the moment that heaven allowed His last breath. No one took His life from Him, He laid it down by Himself.

His work on earth was complete. He had been obedient to death. He had glorified His Father in heaven.

Now it was the day of Preparation, and the next day was to be a special Sabbath. Because the Jews did not want the bodies left on the crosses during the Sabbath, they asked Pilate to have the legs broken and the bodies taken down. 19:31

The Jewish leaders still haven't peace of mind. It's not enough that they succeeded in having Jesus killed – now they insist his body must be taken down from the cross. So Pilate gives the usual order.

The soldiers therefore came and broke the legs of the first man who had been crucified with Jesus, and then those of the other.
But when they came to Jesus and found that he was already dead, they did not break his legs.
Instead, one of the soldiers pierced Jesus' side with a spear, bringing a sudden flow of blood and water. 19:32-34

In an act of savage violence one of the soldiers launches his spear into the side of Jesus. It was gratuitous violence. Violence for violence's sake. There was no need for it.

In his reporting John makes no attempt to explain the flow of blood and water from Jesus' side. He sees something that he must remind us about:

The man who saw it has given testimony, and his testimony is true.
He knows that he tells the truth, and he testifies so that you also may believe.
These things happened so that the scripture would be fulfilled: "Not one of his bones will be broken," and, as another scripture says, "They will look on the one they have pierced." 19:35-37

Jesus sacrifice was unique.
All the sacrifices of the ages were gathered up and rendered obsolete for ever.
There is therefore now no more sacrifice for sins forever.

John 19:38-42

THE BURIAL OF JESUS

As we conclude this chapter notice

THE SERVICE OF THOSE WHO TOOK HIM DOWN FROM THE CROSS.

Pilate had another visitor that afternoon.

This time, one of Jesus' friends.

Later, Joseph of Arimathea asked Pilate for the body of Jesus.

Now Joseph was a disciple of Jesus, but secretly because he feared the Jews. With Pilate's permission, he came and took the body away.19:38

Perhaps he was among those mentioned in John 12:42.

Yet at the same time many even among the leaders believed in him. But because of the Pharisees they would not confess their faith for fear they would be put out of the synagogue; for they loved praise from men more than praise from God. 12:42-43

He seems to have decided that he can remain a secret disciple no longer. With considerable courage he goes to Pilate and requests that Jesus' body, now the property of Rome, be released to him for burial. His request was granted.

There was blessing for another secret disciple in Joseph's action.

He was accompanied by Nicodemus, the man who earlier had vis-ited Jesus at night. Nicodemus brought a mixture of myrrh and aloes, about seventy-five pounds. 19:39

So at least four loving hands took Jesus' body down from the cross.

Taking Jesus' body, the two of them wrapped it, with the spices, in strips of linen. This was in accordance with Jewish burial customs. At the place where Jesus was crucified, there was a garden, and in the garden a new tomb, in which no-one had ever been laid. Because it was the Jewish day of Preparation and since the tomb was nearby, they laid Jesus there. 19:40-42

Thank God for those timorous disciples, who when they were needed, came out of the shadows and performed the last offices for One they loved.

Thank You, Heavenly Father:

For John's faithful reporting of the events surrounding the death of Jesus, including his burial-place and the Jewish customs that were observed. The body of Jesus was treated with the utmost dignity and respect and for this we are very grateful;

For the amount of spiritual revelation that the Jews were allowed to see and hear about Jesus, whom they knew had called himself the Son of God, and yet none had the courage to confess openly and truthfully what some were thinking about him. Heavenly Father, if we may think aloud in your presence, we wonder if any (or many) of them were present and witnessed the events of the Day of Pentecost when the

Holy Spirit came and some 3,000 souls were born again and added to the Christian Church;

For all those whose lives had been touched by the ministry of Jesus for the previous three and a half years of his ministry or preaching, teaching and he aling.

In Jesus' Name, Amen.

A RECOMMENDATION
TO MY READERS:

I want to recommend a wonderful Easter hymn to your attention. I have both words and music at home. You will understand I am not free to publish it in my Manuscript without the permission of the Copyright holders.

The hymn is: *'Yes finished! the Messiah dies'*
In some older books: *'Tis finished! The Messiah dies'*
This hymn was written by Rev. Charles Wesley and to my delight has appeared in a new hymn book entitled
'PRAISE HYMNS.

I am very keen that every one of you has access to this hymn. Therefore I recommend searching for it via the Internet – you will find various websites that exist for no other reason than to make hymns accessible.

Following your internet searches try finding the hymn by asking local church organists and other musicians.

Perhaps they will know the hymn and may allow you to access the words and music, or purchase a copy of 'PRAISE HYMNS' of your own. There are both words and music editions available. JRG

JOHN 20:

LORD OF THE EMPTY TOMB

When you first discover Canon Michael Saward's hymn: *'Lord of the Cross of Shame'* you possibly think *'what an incredibly beautiful hymn.'*

Then, moving into verse 2 we wonder where the writer is going. He appears to begin well: *'Lord of the Empty Tomb'* but in the next line he goes straight to our Lord's incarnation: *'born of a virgin's womb.'* When we read on through the verse we discover that he has not lost his way, but rather has laid the foundation for what is to follow!

> **'Lord of the empty tomb,**
> **born of a virgin's womb,**
> **triumphant over death, its power defeated;**
> **how gladly now I sing**
> **Your praise, my Risen King,**
> **and worship You, in heaven's splendour seated.'**

The body that was given to Jesus at his conception was the body that was nailed to the cross, died on the cross and was taken down from the cross and laid in a tomb. But he didn't stay dead.

On the first Easter Sunday morning Jesus rose from the tomb and lives today in the power of an endless life. No one saw Him rise and emerge from the tomb – but hundreds of people met the Risen Christ. He appeared to them and so they had first hand, personal experience of meeting Him.

All these facts are reasons to worship Jesus, our Risen King where He is now *'in heaven's splendour seated.'*

The title for this study is
John 20: JESUS: LORD of the Empty Tomb

So far, we have found the section headings in the NIV Bible appropriate and fairly accurate – so we shall continue to use them.

20:1-9   THE EMPTY TOMB
20:10-18 JESUS APPEARS TO MARY MAGDALENE
20:19-23 JESUS APPEARS TO HIS DISCIPLES
20:24-31 JESUS APPEARS TO THOMAS.

This is a key chapter in the history of Christianity.
It is brimful of facts.
Christianity rests on facts,
the facts of a Saviour's life, death, burial,
resurrection, ascension and his personal return in glory.

JOHN 20:1-9

THE EMPTY TOMB

**The emphasis of this chapter is that the
resurrection is historical.
<u>It happened in space and time</u>.
The space was the tomb of Joseph of Arimathea;
the time was 'the first day of the week' following
Passover in the year 33 AD.**

*Early on the first day of the week, while it was still dark, Mary
Magdalene went to the tomb and saw that the stone had been
removed from the entrance.* 20:1

Why had she gone there? She was the first of a group
of women who had been at the tomb on Friday evening around 6 o'clock – who intended to return and complete
the embalming process on the body of Jesus. The thought of a
bodily resurrection was furthest from her mind.

The visit was made very early *'while it was still dark'*. v. 1

Whatever she was thinking of she was non-plussed when she
saw that the stone had been removed from the entrance to the
tomb. She may have not been alone because when speaking to
Peter she used the plural *'we'*.

So she came running to Simon Peter and the other disciple, the one Jesus loved, and said,

"They have taken the Lord out of the tomb, and __we__ don't know where they have put him!" 20:2

In her alarm she decided to get help—*so she ran to find Peter and John.* She must have had some confidence in Peter despite his recent denials of Jesus. When she said *'we don't know where __they__ have put him'*—who was she thinking might have interfered with the tomb?

Peter and John also express alarm and decided to go and see for themselves. *So Peter and the other disciple started for the tomb.* 20:3

John the younger man outran Peter and got there first.

Both were running, but the other disciple outran Peter and reached the tomb first. 20:4-5

On arriving at the tomb the two men acted differently.

He (John) bent over and looked in at the strips of linen lying there but did not go in.

John hesitated outside. What did Peter do? Read on.

Then Simon Peter, who was behind him, arrived and went into the tomb.
He saw the strips of linen lying there, as well as the burial cloth that had been around Jesus' head. The cloth was folded up by itself, separate from the linen. 20:6-7

Neither found any evidence of the tomb being disturbed. In fact they found the grave-clothes well-nigh undisturbed as though Jesus' body had simply passed through them – in much the same way as he later entered and/or left locked rooms. The head turban lay a little distance away, folded by itself, separate from the linen.

> *Finally the other disciple, who had reached the tomb first, also went inside.* ***He saw and believed.***
> *(They still did not understand from Scripture that Jesus had to rise from the dead.)* 20:8-9

The orderly scene, with the grave-clothes tidily laid aside because of no further use, clinched the matter for John and he believed that Jesus had risen.

For the time being neither man could recall nor did they understand that the assurance they needed was in the Scriptures.

I want to make a number of observations.

1. **John saw the empty tomb with the folded grave clothes no longer in use – <u>AND BELIEVED THAT JESUS HAD RISEN FROM THE DEAD</u>. vv. 1-2.**

JOHN 20:10-18

JESUS APPEARS TO MARY MAGDALENE

Then the disciples went back to their homes, but Mary stood out-side tomb crying. As she wept, she bent over to look into the tomb and saw two angels in white, seated where Jesus' body had been, one at the head and the other at the foot.

Then she was aware of someone speaking to her:

<u>*"Woman,"*</u> he said, <u>*"why are you crying?*</u>

<u>*Who is it you are looking for?"*</u>

Thinking he was the gardener, she said,

"Sir, if you have carried him away, tell me where you have put him, and I will get him." 20:14-15

Jesus said to her, *"Mary."*

She turned towards him and cried out in Aramaic,

"Rabboni!" (which means Teacher). 20:16

2. **Mary Magdalene recognised Jesus' voice when he spoke her name, and responded with immediate recognition of who he was (rabboni = *'my dear teacher'*). <u>SHE BELIEVED JESUS HAD RISEN FROM THE DEAD,</u> vv. 10-16**

I t only took a single word spoken by the Risen Lord – his mention of her by name – and she knew it was him! She is ecstatic at the sound. She had often heard Him call her name.

WHY DID SHE NOT RECOGNISE HIM SOONER? Unlike Lazarus who had to be resuscitated, Jesus had passed through death and was now part of a new order of life in the glory of His Father's presence.

Jesus said, *"Do not hold on to me, for I have not yet returned to the Father. Go instead to my brothers and tell them, 'I am returning to my Father and your Father, to my God and your God.' "*

Mary Magdalene went to the disciples with the news: *"I have seen the Lord!" And she told them that he had said these things to her.* 20:17-18

There are two possibilities here:
(1) Mary don't hold on to me as if you will never see me again! This will not be My only appearance to you and the others.
(2) From now on, although resurrection appearances are a special exception, you will not relate to me by touch and by sight. We shall have a new, by-faith, relationship. 'I will be closer to you than breathing, closer than hands and feet.'

Jesus had given her a message to deliver to the other disciples;

Go instead to my brothers and tell them, 'I am returning to my Father and your Father, to my God and your God.'

Possibly Jesus had yet to ascend to heaven to appear in the presence of His Father (and theirs) and to His God (and theirs). There is the possibility of Jesus moving freely between heaven and earth in His glorified resurrection body: *i.e. prior to His ascension in Acts 1:9.*

JOHN 20:19-23

JESUS APPEARS TO HIS DISCIPLES

On the evening of that first day of the week, when the disciples were together, with the doors locked for fear of the Jews, Jesus came and stood among them and said, "Peace be with you!"
After he said this, he showed them his hands and side. The disciples were overjoyed when they saw the Lord. 20:19-20

I n our hurting world, it is a privilege to point men and women to the Lord Jesus Christ, and tell them that Jesus is recognised by his scars. Hence they will not be lead astray by imposters.

3. **JESUS' DISCIPLES BELIEVED HE HAD RISEN FROM THE DEAD** **when he entered the locked room where they were meeting and showed them his wounded hands and his side. 19-25**

But we are not quite finished with this section. Vv. 21-23 follow.

Again Jesus said, "Peace be with you! As the Father has sent me, I am sending you."
And with that he breathed on them and said, "Receive the Holy Spirit. If you forgive anyone his sins, they are forgiven; if you do not forgive them, they are not forgiven." 20:21-23

God is a missionary God.
He had only one Son and He made Him a missionary.
The disciples of Jesus are meant to be missionaries,
beginning with the apostles.
Another thing: Who can forgive sins but God alone?'
It is not part of a pastor or evangelists' responsibility
to forgive sin.
The Reformers understood vv. 22 & 23 as follows:
'the loosing' and 'binding' occur
when the Gospel is preached
around the world. It is in response to the Gospel that
sinners find forgiveness with God.

20:24-31 JESUS APPEARS TO THOMAS.

Now Thomas (called Didymus), one of the Twelve, was not with
the disciples when Jesus came.
So the other disciples told him, "We have seen the Lord!"
But he said to them, "Unless I see the nail marks in his hands and
put my finger where the nails were, and put my hand into his side,
I will not believe it." 20:24-25

Recall what Thomas' colleagues had just said to him. *We have seen the Lord!"* Does his response reveal doubt or merely a desire to share a similar experience to theirs?

John is preparing his readers for some more good news. It happened on the second Sunday evening following the Passover.

A week later his disciples were in the house again, and Thomas was with them. Though the doors were locked, Jesus came and stood among them and said, "Peace be with you!"

Then he said to Thomas, "Put your finger here; see my hands. Reach out your hand and put it into my side. Stop doubting and believe."
Thomas said to him, "My Lord and my God!" 20:26-28

Jesus had entered the room in His post-resurrection manner – through locked doors.

He had come for Thomas' sake – and gave him a unique invitation.

In the event Thomas didn't have to touch the wounds of Jesus. He simply uttered words of pure worship: *"My Lord and my God!"* And his confession was accepted without question.

4. <u>**THOMAS BELIEVED THAT JESUS HAD RISEN FROM THE DEAD**</u> **when he entered the locked room where the disciples were meeting, spoke to Thomas by name, and invited him to touch his wounded hands and side. vv. 26-29**

Thomas became the only believer in the New Testament records to address Jesus with these words. Jesus accepted his worship.

Those who did not have Thomas' privilege of standing before Jesus in that Upper Room in Jerusalem, looking on His wounds and into His face, are not inferior to him in Christian experience.

Jesus made this abundantly clear in what follows:

Then Jesus told him, "Because you have seen me, you have believed; blessed are those who have not seen and yet have believed." **20:29**

308

This is the point in a good book where you find yourself screaming at the author:

DON'T STOP HERE!

John 20: 30-31

THE PURPOSE OF JOHN'S GOSPEL

Jesus did many other miraculous signs in the presence of his disciples, which are not recorded in this book. But these are written that you may believe that Jesus is the Christ, the Son of God, and that by believing you may have life in his name. 20:30-31

Thank You, Heavenly Father:

We claim the promise that Jesus gave to his disciple Thomas
(20:2): Because you have seen me, you have believed;
blessed are those who have not seen and yet have believed;

We have tried to enter into the sufferings of Jesus on his way
to the cross, and his death on the cross, and have found it
impossible to imagine his experience; we have never experienced any physical or spiritual suffering that comes anywhere near to it. 'There was no sorrow like unto his sorrow.'

We cannot doubt, nor is there any shadow of doubt about the
sufficiency of the sacrifice that Jesus offered in atonement
for our sins at Calvary where 'he took my sins and my sorrows and made them his very own.'

In Jesus' Name, Amen.

John 21

LORD OF MY LIFE TODAY

21:1-14 Jesus and the miraculous catch of fish.
21:15-25 Jesus reinstates Peter.

E aster Sunday, and the Sunday following, would remain in the memories of the apostles and the other disciples for a very long time.

There had never been days like these before – memorable for the fact that Jesus Christ had shown himself alive from the dead.

However, the best of days is only 24 hours long!
What then? The short answer is that life has to go on!

That is the style of John chapter 21 – as the disciples adjusted to their new relationship with their Risen Lord. It appears that He wasn't expecting them to go with Him as in the years leading up to His death and resurrection. So naturally some of them, who were fishermen, returned to their trade. Their relationship and loyalty to Jesus had not changed – it will be worked out differently in future.

Our friend, Canon Michael Saward, caught this mood in a masterly way in the third and final verse of his hymn.

<u>Lord of my life today</u>

teach me to live and pray

as on who knows the joy of sins forgiven;

so may I ever be,

now and eternally,

one with my fellow-citizens of heaven.

That is a beautiful and appropriate name for believers to use when speaking to Jesus in praise and prayer.

I cannot think of a more practical theme

with which to close this series of studies in John's gospel.

However, before we move on, there is another important observation to make about this chapter viz. it seems to serve the important task of recording the rehabilitation of Peter.

I think we should be grateful for this. The years have passed since Peter denied his Lord in the Courtyard of the High Priest in Jerusalem. John was an elderly man by the time he wrote this gospel. It's good to know that the best years of Peter's Christian service lay in between *then* and *now*!

Within the broad section headings of the NIV-UK I want to emphasise some practical matters affecting you and me.

Afterwards Jesus appeared again to his disciples, by the Sea of Tiberias. It happened this way.
Simon Peter, Thomas (called Didymus), Nathanael from Cana in Galilee, the sons of Zebedee, and two other disciples were together.
"I'm going out to fish," Simon Peter told them, and they said, "We'll go with you." So they went out and got into the boat, but that night they caught nothing. 21:1-3

One very experienced commentator (and principal of a Theological College) is reported as having said: 'Never has a fishing trip been so severely judged! I expect that he was bored to death by generations of students evaluating the reasons why some of the disciples resorted to fishing at this point in their lives.

At least one of these men owned a boat, and so they went out to fish all night, as they had done hundreds, perhaps thousands, of times before.

I think that the obvious practical reason for this fishing expedition was that, until they discovered or were told what the Risen Lord wanted them to do – they simply went back to their trade. For this I commend them.

The result of this fishing trip will be that Peter, who knew Jesus as Lord of the cross of shame, and Lord of the empty tomb, will learn that Jesus is Lord of his life today. He is going to learn that Jesus is Lord of every area of his life.

So far as Jesus was concerned in what was about to unfold He considered Himself as Lord of Peter's daily occupation. This is point 1 in the chapter.

1. JESUS is LORD of PETER'S DAILY OCCUPATION.
vv 1-14 See how He directs him!

Early in the morning, Jesus stood on the shore, but the disciples did not realise that it was Jesus.
*He called out to them, "**Friends, haven't you any fish?**"*
*"**No**," they answered.*
*He said, "**Throw your net on the right side of the boat and you will find some.**"*

313

When they did, they were unable to haul the net in because of the large number of fish. 21:4-6

Fishermen are not renowned for taking advice from strangers, particularly one still on land. Somehow they are not in the mood for an argument and so they act on the advice given. Suddenly they are hauling in a miraculous catch of fish.

That stimulated their memories. John knew who it was on the shore. For him it was another moment of revelation. (v. 7)

Then the disciple whom Jesus loved said to Peter, "It is the Lord!" As soon as Simon Peter heard him say, "It is the Lord," he wrapped his outer garment around him (for he had taken it off) and jumped into the water. 21:7

For Peter it was a summons to action. Peter was only lightly clothed so he pulled on his over-garment and tucked it up around him so as not to impede his movement.

The other disciples followed in the boat, towing the net full of fish, for they were not far from shore, about a hundred yards. 21:8

For whatever reason, Peter abandoned the catch of fish and went ashore. There he found a strange sight:

When they landed, they saw a fire of burning coals there with fish on it, and some bread.
Jesus said to them, "Bring some of the fish you have just caught."
21:9-10

Jesus was ahead of them all in his thinking. These men would be hungry – so he prepared a fire with fish and bread already on it! He invited Peter to add some fish from the night's catch.

Simon Peter climbed aboard and dragged the net ashore. It was full
of large fish, 153, but even with so many the net was not torn. 21:11

They had caught no less than 153 whoppers! Perhaps some
of them were doing multiplication sums in their heads about
how much the fish would sell for in the local market.

Jesus said to them, "Come and have breakfast."
None of the disciples dared ask him, "Who are you?"
They knew it was the Lord.
Jesus came, took the bread and gave it to them, and did the same
with the fish. 21:12-13

So the men ate what He gave them and the very sharing of
the meal was a further unveiling of His presence.

This was now the third time Jesus appeared to his disciples after
he was raised from the dead. 21:14

I don't think that I have to labour the point to help us all to
realise that whether we are employers or employees, if we call
ourselves by Christ's name then Jesus is LORD of our Daily
Occupation.

You will know that the majority of the New Testament letters have two parts: a general and/or doctrinal section which is
followed by another practical section. '*Where the rubber hits*
*the ro*ad' as they say in the motor trade. The pastor might put it
differently: '*where the doctrine hits the road.*'

The Spirit clothed himself with Gideon
He makes the record say;
So he became the working clothes
The Spirit wore that day.

2. JESUS is LORD of PETER'S CHRISTIAN PROFESSION.

vv. 15-19 See how He restores him.

This seems to have been the first opportunity since the resurrection for Jesus and Peter to have a confidential chat.

Peter had professed, ever so strongly that however others behaved, the Lord could always rely on him. 13:36-38

But, alas, Peter had denied his Lord, most shamefully, not once, not twice, but three times.18:25-27

Now, very quietly, very gently, Jesus asks Peter a few pointed, personal questions.

When they had finished eating, Jesus said to Simon Peter,
"Simon son of John, do you truly love me more than these?"
"Yes, Lord," he said, "you know that I love you."
Jesus said, "Feed my lambs." 21:15

Jesus used Peter's old name!
'Simon' Do you truly love me?

Again Jesus said,
"Simon son of John, do you truly love me?
He answered, *"Yes, Lord, you know that I love you.*
Jesus said, *"Take care of my sheep."* 21:16
The third time he said to him,
"Simon son of John, do you love me?"
Peter was hurt because Jesus asked him the third time,
"Do you love me?"
He said, *"Lord, you know all things; you know that I love you."*
Jesus said, *"Feed my sheep.* 21:17

Jesus has given Peter an opportunity to undo his denials with these three reaffirmations of love and loyalty to his Lord. This not the place for a Greek lesson about the words for *'love'* that Jesus and Peter used.

It is the place to point out that Jesus accepts what we are able to give Him.

Peter was being utterly honest with Jesus –
and with himself!

This is the key-issue for each of us in our relationship with Jesus Christ: can we affirm that

JESUS IS LORD OF OUR CHRISTIAN PROFESSION.

Next the emphasis shifts to Peter's future.

3. JESUS is LORD of PETER'S FUTURE SERVICE
vv. 20-23 See how He counsels him.

Having accepted a renewed commission from Jesus (vv 15-17) there is something else that Peter needs to know. Jesus now prepares Peter for what the commission will cost him. He has something far-reaching to say to Peter.

> *I tell you the truth, when you were younger you dressed yourself and went where you wanted; but when you are old you will stretch out your hands, and someone else will dress you and lead you where you do not want to go."*

Jesus said this to indicate the kind of death by which Peter would glorify God. 21:18-19
Then he said to him, "Follow me!"
Jesus is looking down the years to Peter's eventual martyrdom.

That *'follow me'* at the end of v. 19 is all important.

Peter turned and saw that the disciple whom Jesus loved was following them. (This was the one who had leaned back against Jesus at the supper and had said, "Lord, who is going to betray you?")
When Peter saw him, he asked, "Lord, what about him?" 21:20-21
Jesus answered, "If I want him to remain alive until I return, what is that to you? You must follow me." 21:22-23

We can bracket the next sentence: *(Because of this, the rumour spread among the brothers that this disciple would not die. But Jesus did not say that he would not die; he only said, "If I want him to remain alive until I return, what is that to you?")*

I don't know which is worse:
PLAYING GOD with other people's lives?
Or PLAYING GOD with our own lives?
Sometimes people come to their pastor/minister
and say I don't know what God wants me to do?
Possibly they don't realise how big that question is.
They are tempting their pastor to 'play God' with them.
Sometime their pastors do that!
It takes honesty and courage to say:
'I don't know what God's will is for your life'.
But, I will pray with you now that God will reveal that to you
in His own time and way.
What about the temptation to 'play God'
with your own life?
We have everything mapped out (and under our breath say)
'There you are Lord, now you know what I want!
Friends, do you ever wonder:-

'How does God get anything done?'

'You ask me what forgiveness means?

it is the wonder of being trusted again by God

in the place where I disgraced Him.'

<u>Rita Snowden.</u>

Why not sing with Michael Saward?

'How gladly now I sing

Your praise my Risen King,

and worship You, in heaven's splendour seated

Thank You, Heavenly Father,

For the realisation that the Lord of the cross of shame, and *Lord of the empty tomb and the Lord of my life today* is one and the same glorious person, able to save to the uttermost all who come to God through him;

For the privilege of serving such a Master, who modelled everything he ever asked of his disciples to do; there is no situation that we meet in his service that he has not met the equal of it;

For the joy that Jesus has set before us that will be realised in whole-hearted Christian service and when he shall come again.

For the ability of our risen and ascended Lord to keep us from falling and to present us before his glorious presence without fault and with great joy;

To You, the only God our Saviour be glory, majesty, power and authority, through Jesus Christ our Lord, before all ages, now and forevermore!

In Jesus' Name, Amen.

Lightning Source UK Ltd.
Milton Keynes UK
UKOW06f1848010515

250769UK00003B/5/P